What people are saying about ...

While the rest of us are unsettled by the shifting business landscape created by technology, Jim Blasingame has been doing the deep thinking about how to turn frustrating disruptions into opportunities. With his new book, The Age of The Customer, *you and I become the beneficiaries of the insights Jim has achieved, including what is happening, why, and how we can lead this change, instead of reacting to it.*

Steven C. Martin
President, Business Solutions—The Positive Way

Jim Blasingame delivers powerful prose, poignant examples, and practical advice in his new book, The Age of the Customer. *A wake-up call for every business manager, Jim will help you understand how to meet your customers' expanded expectations of value and relevance. If you only read two books this year, read this one twice!*

Chip R. Bell
Author of *The 9½ Principles of Innovative Service*

More than ever, customers control the destiny of your business. In chapter 2 of Jim Blasingame's new book, The Age of The Customer, *the side-by-side images reveal this truth with maximum impact and minimum words. Jim delivers his refreshing message without tech jargon or meaningless platitudes. This book is full of rich information and a road map to help you navigate the new age—the Age of the Customer.*

Ramon Ray
Editor & Technology Evangelist, Smallbiztechnology.com

In The Age of the Customer, *Jim Blasingame explains how control has shifted from businesses to customers. This isn't a book about technology; rather why and how your customers are expecting more. Jim's analysis is well-earned from conversations with business owners, experts, economists, and analysts every working day for more than two decades. The good news for readers of his new book is, he listened.*

Ted C. Fishman
Author of *Shock of Gray* and *China, Inc.*

Jim Blasingame has a gift for surfing the world's most innovative edges while staying grounded in common sense and timeless truths. The Age of the Customer *is chock-full of guideposts, tips, and tools to help you skillfully act on what Jim will teach you. This book will transform how you think about the future of your business.*

John Bradberry
Author of *Six Secrets to Start-up Success*

In his new book, Jim Blasingame has produced the first ever coherent manifesto on how your business will survive and thrive in the new reality he reveals as the Age of the Customer. In plain language, Jim helps you navigate the noisy free-for-all of global, mobile communities of newly empowered customers and influencers. Ignore the mind-changing truths of this book at your peril.

Stephen H. Baum
Coach to CEOs
Author of *What Made jack welch Jack Welch*

It's rare that a book can so thoroughly define what is coming next. Jim Blasingame's new book has done this by combining years of interviewing leading-edge thinkers with his own astute analysis and foresight. In The Age of the Customer, *Jim clearly delivers details and stories that illuminate how the marketplace is changing like never before.*

Joel Barker
Futurist, filmmaker, author

If you feel like things are happening to you and your business instead of you being in charge, this book is what you're looking for. In The Age of the Customer, *Jim Blasingame makes the enormously complex marketplace understandable, and then he delivers action steps for your success today and in the future.*

Peter Meyer
Author of *Creating and Dominating New Markets*

Jim Blasingame says customers are changing the rules in a way that's never happened before. In his new book, he explains how this is happening, how to avoid missing the signals, and the steps to take to be a change leader. Jim is the best at telling such a Big Idea story in plain language.

Hector Barreto
Chairman, The Latino Coalition
Former Administrator, U.S. Small Business Administration

The way business is done is changing. In The Age of the Customer, *Jim Blasingame walks you through what is causing the changes and guides you to become a successful leader of this change instead of being run over by it. This book is a must read for anyone in business.*

Robert Levin
Founder, *New York Enterprise Report*

In The Age of the Customer, *Jim Blasingame beautifully delivers stories about how customer expectations are influenced by high-tech tools while simultaneously seeking high-touch values and relevance. If you want to significantly increase the ability of your business to deliver on these complex customer expectations, read Jim's new book and adopt his Laws.*

Patricia Greene
Professor of Entrepreneurship, Babson College

With his new book, The Age of the Customer, *Jim Blasingame helps you understand why customers now have more control and why it's not getting any easier to acquire and keep them. In his consistently entertaining way—including real-world examples and true stories—Jim reveals the new things your customers are thinking about. This book won't go on a shelf; you'll keep it handy.*

Paul Sarvadi
Chairman and CEO, Insperity

This book is fantastic! The Age of the Customer *is a powerful perspective on the transformation that is happening in the relationship between businesses and customers. Told in classic Blasingame style, this amazing work is a must-read for student and seasoned business owner alike.*

Giovanni Coratolo
Vice President, Small Business Policy, U.S. Chamber of Commerce

Don't be fooled by Jim Blasingame's ability to deliver a very readable and enjoyable book. Jim is a big intellect and deep thinker, with prodigious experience talking with global business leaders as well as small business owners. His accurate summary of how the power of trust is impacting the Age of the Customer is just one of the reasons why you will love and benefit from this book.

Arky Ciancutti, M.D.
Chairman, Learning Center, Inc.
Co-author of *Built on Trust*

In The Age of the Customer, *Jim Blasingame identifies forces that are creating the greatest seismic marketplace shifts in the history of business since the invention of money. Jim also shows you how this disruption is changing the expectations of your customers. The answers to why you may be feeling this disruption, and how to turn it into opportunity, are in this book.*

John F. Dini
Business owner coach
Author of *Hunting in a Farmer's World*

In Jim Blasingame's new book, his goal is not to make you comfortable, but to help you succeed in this new and challenging world of business. This book, with its helpful stories and persuasive line of reasoning, is the boot camp manual to help you succeed in the new Age of the Customer.

Burton Folsom, Jr.
Author of *New Deal or Raw Deal*

In his new book, Jim Blasingame delivers shrewd insights into a major marketplace shift: the Age of the Customer. Jim has no peer as a passionate champion of small business and a rare source of folksy marketplace intelligence. You need to know what he knows.

Rick Newman
Columnist, *Yahoo! Finance*
Author of *Rebounders: How Winners Pivot from Setback to Success*

Not a moment too soon, Jim Blasingame has produced the guide you need to do business in the Age of the Customer, as the marketplace power shifts from businesses to customers. Jim's new book is filled with insight, perspective, and practical advice from a guy who really knows business. Well done, Jim.

Kirk Cheyfitz
CEO + Chief Storyteller, Story Worldwide

In his new book, The Age of the Customer, *Jim Blasingame does for business what Thomas Friedman did for globalization in his book,* The World is Flat. *He's combined behaviors and trends in one place, and explains them so we can see them more clearly, how they're impacting our business, and what steps to take. And Jim's writing style makes it easy to read; just like you're having a conversation with a really smart friend.*

Anita Rosen
President of ReadyGo, Inc.
Internet pioneer, online expert, author

He's done it again! In his new book, Jim Blasingame has brought us back to the prime fundamental of all business—discovering what customers expect from us. Only this time, he's revealed how the Age of the Customer is altering customer expectations, why we may be missing these signals, and how to get reconnected at the Moment of Relevance. Good job, Jim!"

Andrew J. Sherman
Partner, Jones Day
Author of *Harvesting Intangible Assets*

In his well-written, down-to-earth new book The Age of the Customer, *Jim Blasingame proves that business sustainability is not just about the environment. By broadening the definition to include engaging and encouraging the new power and expanded expectations of customers, Jim shows you the way to a new level of business sustainability.*

Bruce Piasecki
President of the AHC Group
Author of *Doing More with Less: The New Way to Wealth*

To get the attention of leaders of small and mid-size businesses you have to be informative, entertaining, and real. In his new book, The Age of the Customer, *Jim Blasingame delivers all three, with several strong challenges thrown in for good measure. If you're responsible for the future success of your business, this book will help you.*

Mick Fleming
President, American Chamber of Commerce Executives

The future success of every business owner will require preparing for the opportunities and disruptions Jim Blasingame reveals in his new book, The Age of the Customer. *No one does it better than Jim.*

Stephen Moore
Economics writer
Author of *Who's the Fairest of Them All?*

The Age of the Customer®

Prepare for the Moment of Relevance™

Jim Blasingame

The AGE of the CUSTOMER

PREPARE FOR THE MOMENT OF RELEVANCE

Jim Blasingame

FOREWORD BY STEVE FORBES

The Age of the Customer

Prepare for the Moment of Relevance

 For information, contact SBN BOOKS, 503 E. Tuscaloosa St., Florence, AL 35630. SBN BOOKS is a Small Business Network, Inc. company.

Printed in the United States of America

10 9 8 7 6 5 4 3 2 1

Publisher's Cataloging-in-Publication

(Provided by Quality Books, Inc.)

Blasingame, Jim.

The age of the customer : prepare for the moment of relevance / Jim Blasingame ; foreword by Steve Forbes.

pages. cm.

Includes bibliographical references and index.

ISBN 978-0-9709278-2-8 (hardcover)

ISBN 978-0-9709278-3-5 (e-book)

1. Small business—Management. 2. Entrepreneurship. 3. Success in business. I. Title.

HF5386.B53 2013 658.4'09

QBI13-600146

To Davonna, my partner in life and business.
I'm the reason we get invited to go places;
you're the reason we get invited to go back.

Other books by Jim Blasingame

Small Business Is Like a Bunch of Bananas
Three Minutes to Success

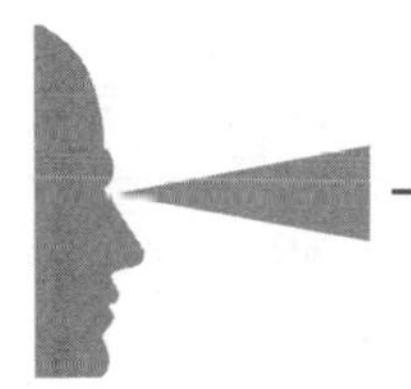

Acknowledgements

Having finished my third book, and in my work as a radio talk show host, interviewing hundreds of authors over the years, I've arrived at this conclusion: Writing and publishing a book is as close as a man can get to birthing a baby. And just like that natural process, no author can produce a book by himself.

Indeed, there are many contributors to this book. From inspiration to perspiration, and execution to distribution, the list of my co-parents is long and varied: prophets and fellow heretics, thought-leaders and subject-matter experts, critics and safe-harbors, passive and aggressive reviewers, gentle editors and sociopathic ones you never, ever feed after midnight.

The only thing more important than for your work to have meaning is for your life to have meaning. In my world, one person is the nexus for both: my partner in life and business. Davonna, no one has ever helped me define meaning like you have. Without your critical contribution and abiding devotion, this book would not have happened. I'm proud of you and I'm proud of us.

Over the life of this book, a number of my team members have contributed, including some who've moved on to other opportunities and some who are still in the trenches with me. Thanks to Lonnie Crawford, Cole Pearson, and Ethan Voce, who made important early contributions to content and appearance. Tyler Martin, you arrived later, but will play an important role in this book's digital life. And Amanda Millwood, thanks for your skills and strong will as an editor and generational filter. Kevin Burgess, the professional way you've contributed to the production of my radio program, especially the extra effort during the period of writing this book, was critical and is much appreciated.

My editor is Jennifer Read Hawthorne, who just happens to also be a member of my Brain Trust. Jennifer, thanks for your professional contribution to making my book better in spite of its author. And I'm in your debt for caring enough about my work to go best-two-falls-out-of-three with me when I needed to be dragged, kicking and screaming, to a better result. Also thanks to Laura Weinberg for her excellent proofreading contribution.

For more than 20 years, my business's best friend has been the professionals at First Metro Bank. Without your support in helping me manage the constant capital challenges facing every small business, I wouldn't have made it. Community banks rock!

One of the people who contributed to this book, without really knowing it at the time, is Jay Mincks. Jay, thanks for being one of the best executives I've ever known and for helping me forge some of my ideas in a real-world environment. If a steady, ethical bearing and servant-leadership are measures of a man among men, you're a giant.

And thanks to our many business partners who contributed essential services, especially the folks at Aha! A Creative Agency and Bang Printing.

Whenever I finish a project, especially a significant one, like writing a book, I think of my parents, James and Virginia. You blessed me in many ways, but the two that really stand out in my quest to be a successful small business owner are: allowing me to be a witness as you experienced life's struggles with class, and the way you showed me the nobility of work. Without these two guiding principles, I surely would not have made it. Thanks, Mom. Thanks, Dad.

I'm especially grateful for, and to, my children and grandchildren, who love me anyway.

In previous books I've acknowledged my teachers and professors, whose long-suffering regarding my upbringing was only eclipsed by my own parents. As in the past, I will recognize two of these special people. Mrs. Rose was my second first grade teacher (the first one didn't work out). Thank you, Mrs. Rose for saving me. Dr. Jack Brown, I expected to learn vertebrate zoology from you, but I had no idea how much more you would teach me. Good teachers teach; great teachers, like you, inspire.

The early publishing advice and counsel so generously given by Dan Poynter and Russell Brown continue to pay dividends. Your graciousness inspired and motivated me to repay you by giving back to many other aspiring authors and independent book publishers who have come to me for help, as I did to you all those many years ago.

One of my heroes is legendary, global thought-leader, and tireless champion of free market capitalism, Steve Forbes. Steve, thanks for providing the Foreword for this book, for being a long-time member of my Brain Trust, and especially for your friendship with this small business owner.

Since 1997, I've conducted thousands of live interviews on my radio program with people who are the thought-leaders in their disciplines. To all of those who shared their ideas, vision, and best practices, you contributed greatly to my work on behalf of small businesses. But a very important by-product of all of those conversations is what I learned from you, which has helped me produce this book. To all of my Brain Trust members, some who have been with me for more than 16 years, thank you very much.

But there is a select group of my Brain Trust that I must single out for their special contribution. Of course, Kirk Cheyfitz, whose vision literally gave rise to my idea of the Age of the Customer. Thanks to Joel Barker for your lessons on the power of paradigms, but especially your foresight mentorship. Steve Martin, you've always found a way to put an invaluable mark on my work, and all I have to do is ask. Your time, interest, enormous intellect, and friendship mean a great deal to me.

Thanks to Arky Ciancutti for your guidance on the power of trust. Leslie Kossoff, thanks for how you've helped me convert the big business concept of quality in a way that works for small businesses. Chuck Martin, thanks for your pioneering thought-leadership on the impact of mobile computing. David Dawsey, my IP attorney and Brain Trust member, thanks for keeping me focused on the value of IP for small businesses. Thanks to Doug Barry, with the U.S. Commercial Service, for helping me educate small business owners about trade opportunities. Anita Rosen, thanks for the witness of your experience as an Internet pioneer and contemporary thought-leader.

Others who put their editing mark on my book include Jeff Zbar, Wally Bock, Burt Folsom, Tim Berry, Stephen Baum, John Dini, Ted Fishman, Rob Levin, Peter Meyer, and John Bradberry. Thanks to all of you for your time and interest in making this book better.

Finally, as always, I'm grateful to you, small business owner, for the inspiration you provide me and so many others. Whenever you look in the mirror on those really dark days that all small business owners have, and wonder if your effort, risk, and investment make a difference to anyone, let me emphatically provide the answer. Yes, small business owner, you do make a difference. You matter to your family, to your employees and their families, to your customers, to your community, and to the world.

The work you do is important on so many levels. Your performance aggregates to the sector that creates most of the world's economic output and employment. Your values and what you stand for are a model for how to behave in the marketplace. What's good for small business is good for the world and you demonstrate that model every day.

You do matter, small business owner. And I'm very proud of you for that.

The Small Business Success Attitude

I accept that my small business will face challenges every day. As I begin my day, I will assume the attitude that, regardless of the number of challenges or the degree of difficulty, if my business is to survive, I must face each one. Therefore, I know that the only thing in question today is how well I will respond to challenges, and the future of my business will depend on the answer to that question.

—Jim Blasingame

The Age of the Customer

Prepare for the Moment of Relevance

Table of Contents

Life is divided into three terms—that which was, which is, and which will be. Let us learn from the past to profit by the present, and from the present to live better in the future.

—William Wordsworth

Foreword

We need to promulgate humaneness in business, which is woefully lacking. Too many business people are mercenary and obsessed only with rolling up profits, regardless of the suicidal consequences of their conduct. They are without consciousness of their civic, social, and patriotic responsibilities.

How contemporary do the sentiments in the previous paragraph sound? You may be surprised to learn that this observation of the marketplace was written by my grandfather, B.C. Forbes, almost a century ago. The good news is that these conditions motivated him to start a venture that would produce one of the most trusted business publications in the world, *Forbes* Magazine.

My grandfather published the first edition of *Forbes* in 1917, during what my friend, Jim Blasingame, identifies in this book as the Age of the Seller. Jim describes this as a period when businesses controlled the majority of the elements of their relationships with customers, and the excesses of that control is what my grandfather was concerned about.

One of the great paradoxes we've witnessed in history is how adversity and disruptions often produce better things. Most of the conveniences we enjoy today were envisioned and produced by people who bumped up against a wall of resistance and, refusing to be controlled, innovated an alternative which gave them a path over, under, or around that wall. My grandfather's reaction to greed and bad behavior motivated him to risk everything on a publishing innovation: a business magazine that would advocate and demonstrate the values of humanity, reason, and equity in the marketplace, while promoting free markets.

As Jim points out in this book, technological innovations now empower customers to go over, under, or around the walls of control that businesses enjoyed for millennia. With all of the disruptions this shift is causing businesses—including here at *Forbes*, as we make our journey to convert from print to digital—I think my grandfather would have liked what Jim identifies as the Age of the Customer. He would like seeing how businesses must now work more closely with their two most important stakeholders: customers and employees. He would enjoy seeing businesses reveal and demonstrate their values, as Jim discloses in chapter 7, as part of the bargain they strike to attract and keep customers.

You will learn, as you spend time with Jim in his book, that the most successful way to think about the Age of the Customer is not so much as a shift or disruption, but rather as a reconciliation: Both parties to a transaction, seller and customer, now come together on a more equal footing, where quality and value are partners, competitiveness is trumped by relevance, and transparency is the coin of the realm. This is the new reality of the marketplace in which customers are now inviting businesses, like yours and mine, to participate.

A prophet, it has been said, is someone who foretells the future. And when what is being foretold is not yet our reality, we often indulge our prophets. But foresight is not the only role of a prophet. A true prophet—one with the courage of his convictions—often finds he must also play the role of heretic, which we typically don't indulge.

Jim says a heretic is a true believer with the courage to warn us about complacency with, and the seduction of, the status quo. As you read this book, you'll alternate between seeing Jim as a prophet or a heretic, depending on where you are on your journey of understanding about the transition from the old age to the new one. When you read about ideas Jim reveals that are new to you, he'll be a prophet. But as you begin to realize that what you first thought of as future thinking is actually your here and now, Jim's prophecy will turn to heresy. At that moment, when you start to understand why "the way we've always done it" is no longer producing acceptable results, that's when you must stop resisting and pay the most attention. Because that will be your greatest moment of clarity about the essence of *The Age of the Customer: Prepare for the Moment of Relevance*.

Remember, the blessing of a heretic is tough love. And when it comes to delivering tough love to small business owners, Jim Blasingame is the best. The good news is he's also a great storyteller, which will make his heresy more enjoyable.

One of my grandfather's favorite quotes, which was on the masthead of every *Forbes* magazine for many years is, "With all thy getting, get understanding." I encourage you to allow Jim to help you get the understanding needed to successfully make the transition from your Age of the Seller practices to those that will help you meet the expectations that are now our reality in the Age of the Customer.

Enjoy Jim's book and, in the spirit of B.C. Forbes, I hope you'll promulgate some humaneness in business in the process.

Good luck,

Steve Forbes
Chairman and Editor-in-Chief
Forbes Media

The greatest ability in business is to get along with others and to influence their actions.

—John Hancock

Preface

Since 1997, when I began my syndicated weekday radio program, I started developing relationships with really smart people who became regular guests on my show. This group, which I named the Brain Trust, has become the largest community of small business experts in the world. As thought-leaders in their fields, many of the ideas in this book have been prompted by my conversations with them on my show, as we forged ideas into intellectual alloys that could become useful to others.

One such alloy-forging relationship is with Kirk Cheyfitz, founder and CEO of Story Worldwide, author of *Thinking Inside the Box*, a recovering journalist, and Pulitzer Prize nominee. His expertise is marketing and advertising. Kirk is scary-smart, but the thing that's most endearing is that he's a heretic, like me. A heretic is a true believer who doesn't mind sticking his finger in the eye of the status quo.

Several years ago, during an appearance on my show, Kirk used a term that fascinated me. In describing the current state of the marketing world, he declared that we were in "the post-advertising age."

"Whoa!" I remember thinking. "How can you say that? Especially from your New York City office barely a block away from legendary Madison Avenue, where purveyors of this legacy industry defend the status quo while reading from publications like *Advertising Age*."

Throwing down this gauntlet, Kirk was at once a heretic and a prophet. My immediate reaction was to object to this heresy with a lurch in defense of my multi-decade investment in the status quo. But then the reality I was observing in the bargain that businesses tried to strike with customers, with increasingly diminishing results, whiplashed me over to the power of his prophecy. As the interview continued, it started to become clear to me that Kirk was right. The old way of reaching customers was under indictment for the crime of defaulting on expectations.

As I kept thinking about Kirk's statement over the next several months, my thought process expanded to cause-and-effect: Why is this shift happening? What is causing it? How is it manifesting? Who is it impacting? As I put names to causes and attributed frustrations to effects, I began to see a picture much bigger than advertising and marketing. Kirk's heretical prophecy opened my eyes wider than before and inspired the ideas that have become the essence of this book: the Age of the Seller is being replaced by the Age of the Customer. My vision was now focused on the marketplace writ large, including all practices, paradigms, and people.

In the intervening years between Kirk's post-advertising declaration and the publishing of this book, I developed my focus with articles serialized in my syndication, road testing on my live radio program, and as a keynote speaker in front of live audiences. I hope you will benefit from all of this purifying and hardening of what I believe is an important and valuable alloy that Kirk helped me to forge. It's an alloy that I am convinced you'll need to survive and thrive in the Age of the Customer.

Thanks, Kirk, for the inspiration of your prophecy and the power of your heresy.

And thank you for spending time with me, as we begin this important journey where we'll acknowledge where we've been, establish perspective on where we are, and develop foresight into where we're going.

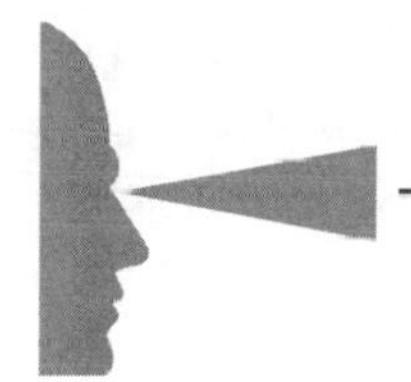

Introduction

And when I die, and when I'm gone,
There'll be one child born
In this world to carry on, to carry on.

—*And When I Die* by Laura Nyro
performed by Blood, Sweat & Tears

It has been said that change is the only constant. Most things are in a constant state of growing and decaying, waxing and waning, living and dying. Each generation gives way to the next; over time, for example, fire evolved into electricity and the wheel morphed into a computer.

But what's happening today is different. We're in the middle of the most dramatic changes in the history of the marketplace. My goal for this book is to help you navigate those changes successfully, and this introduction is designed to lay out my plan.

From the Neolithic era to the end of the 20th century, change in the marketplace was somewhat predictable and manageable. Once upon a time, you could create a marketplace model—a product, strategy, skill, etc.—and expect to make a living off it for a lifetime with little disruption. And for hundreds of family generations, you could even expect to pass a business model on to your children for them to make a living from it.

So if change is so abiding and natural—even predictable—why does it seem there is so much more anxiety about change in the marketplace today than in the past? Well, anxiety is being caused not by change itself, but rather the almost exponential increase in the velocity of change.

Sometime during the 20th century, the marketplace started speeding up to the point where the life expectancy of a typical model generation was compressed into a calendar year. By 1993, the Internet and associated innovations began further compressing time to where a model generation is now measured in Internet terms. What not so long ago could be counted on to be valid for at least a year is now more likely to be obsolete in 90 days. As technology merges time and space, information is delivered faster, knowledge happens quicker, and, as you'll see, customer expectations and what they consider to be relevant to them are changing, sometimes overnight.

What you'll learn in this book is how every business now must buckle up and pull the straps tight, as an unprecedented confluence of innovations has further compressed the time between model generations. Remember, a model generation is the lifespan of a business model, product, campaign, etc., and, in the Age of the Customer, is only valid at the pleasure of your customers' expectations.

A Quick Tour of What's Inside

A golf pro once told me that if you have a bad swing, practicing hard will just reinforce the thing that is producing undesirable results and make you tired and frustrated in the process. Over my career I've observed many businesses becoming tired and frustrated while working hard executing bad and/or obsolete practices. But worse, they're also creating a casualty list that includes employees and, ultimately, the business. The common cause of such drama is a failure by the organization's executives to see the value in foresight practices.

Based on the future they foresee, successful executives develop goals for what they want to accomplish and strategies to make that happen, then give managers those parameters to execute. Regardless of the size of an organization, the expectations of its chief executive officer should include a commitment of time and energy in the disciplines of foresight and strategy. In our time together, I'm going to help you with foresight, strategy, and execution.

If you reduced the concepts of this book to two words, they would be *expectations* and *relevance*—more specifically, *customer expectations of relevance*. Here's the essence of these two ideas in a question every Seller must ask themselves every day: "How can we continually adjust to changes in customer expectations in order to stay relevant to them?"

You'll find the answers to this critical question in Section I:

- Chapter 1, "The Age of the Seller," describes the control model between Seller and Customer for the last 10,000 years. This is a short chapter for a reason—we're at the end of that Age.

- Chapter 2 reveals something that has never happened before. It lays out how a once-in-an-eon paradigm shift in the marketplace power structure has created the Age of the Customer, and how this shift of control is changing the way you do business—now and forever.
- At the new speed of change described above, any business in denial—which I refer to as Hidebound in chapter 3, "Parallel Universes," is likely to start experiencing a heightened level of anxiety and frustration. A successful business model—identified as Visionary in chapter 3—will be one that responds to the increased velocity of change, especially in customer expectations.
- In chapter 4, "Subduction of Expectations," I'll define and provide insight into customer expectations. (This will later be expanded on with practical applications in chapter 12, "Evolution of Expectations.")
- Relevance is so critical to your success in the Age of the Customer that it dominates three chapters. In chapter 5, "The Moment of Relevance," I'll show how relevance is trumping competitiveness and, before we're finished, you'll see how this new coin of the realm is the currency of everything you do in your business in the new Age.
- You'll meet two new groups of Influencers in chapter 6 who are becoming very involved in, and important to, your business—but don't read that as always in a good way.
- In chapter 7, "Value and Values," you'll discover how adding a single letter to the end of a marketplace hallmark announces the birth of a new and powerful differentiator.
- Section I wraps up with chapter 8, "The Power of Trust," where we'll cover how this primordial marketplace-founding force is more powerful in the new Age than ever.

In Section II, each chapter focuses on a practice, behavior, or discipline:

- Chapter 9, "What's Love Got to Do with It?" will help you eject any Age of the Seller baggage that's holding you back.
- Chapters 10 and 11 are devoted to two ways that everything you ever knew about branding, brand ownership, and brand messaging is being disrupted.

- Chapter 12, "Evolution of Expectations," looks at the evolution of customer expectations and how your business practices have to adjust and conform to meet the demands of the new Age.
- In Chapter 13, "Global Mobile," we'll discuss this phenomenon which was not any part of your business's past, but will dominate your future..
- In the new Age, Prospects and Customers are presenting you with a gift I call, "Follow me home," which you'll learn about in chapter 14. And it's not an accident that chapter 15, "Emotional Relevance," is next, nor that chapter 16, "The Rules of Selling Have Changed," and chapter 17 on social media are right behind. These four chapters are designed to help you make the necessary adjustments from Age of the Seller customer acquisition practices to the new rules Customers are expecting from anyone with whom they do business. Did I mention how important chapter 16 is?
- One thing you'll notice is that I've included lots of stories in this book. Some are very short and some not so much. Some stories are woven into the narrative and some are highlighted. Either way you should take away from this that I believe in the power of stories and that your ability to tell them is important to your success in the Age of the Customer. Consequently, I've dedicated chapter 18 to this important topic and followed it up with chapter 19, "You Must Become a Publisher," to help you tell and deliver your stories with the power of new multimedia resources and channels.
- In chapter 20, you'll gain an understanding of how to leverage intellectual property (IP) more and tangible assets less, plus how to combine the IP you create with the kind you acquire from others as components of your growth strategy. And in chapters 21 and 22, respectively, I'll launch you into orbit with the efficient power of cloud computing and then bring you back to Earth by revealing what you cannot do there.
- In chapter 23, I explain how classic quality service must be replaced with the quality process in order to achieve sustainability in the new Age. Next door, in chapter 24, "Outsourcing: The Mother of Niches," I reveal why outsourcing, with its harness mate, technology, are the chicken and egg that birthed the explosion of small business opportunity in the Age of the Customer. And in chapter 25, you'll see why it's time

for more small businesses to look outside the four walls of their business and markets to discover new opportunities in the global economy.

- There are some things that the new Age did not change or disrupt, and I'll remind you of some of those fundamentals in chapter 26, including the two most powerful words in the marketplace.
- And finally, in the Epilogue, I'll really put the arm on you to assume the CEO role of your company by encouraging you to put your futurist hat on and practice the disciplines of executive thinking and foresight.

How to read this book

If you're reading these words, that means I'm preaching to the choir when I encourage you to read the front section of this book. Thank you. But I do hope you'll take the time to see how this book was born, with the story I tell in the Preface. You'll also benefit greatly by reading the introduction to Section I. And who doesn't want to read what Steve Forbes has to say? This will be time well spent, I promise.

Of course, as the creator of all of this brilliance, I want to imagine that you'll begin with word one and not put the book down until the last page. But I'm realistic enough to know that's unlikely, so I'm going to offer a suggestion on how to get the most out of our time together.

Do yourself a favor and read all of Section I before going to any chapter in Section II. The first eight chapters reveal why and how to shed your Age of the Seller baggage, which is essential to success in the new Age. In Section II, the chapters are arranged in groups to some degree, but still, each can stand alone. You should read them once together, but then refer to them, as needed, as individual disciplines become the most pressing issue on any given day.

As you'll see throughout the book, I've coined a number of ideas called, "Blasingame's Laws." I've given these thoughts a name, because they're important nuggets to remember. They're also aggregated them in the back of the book for handy reference.

Please think of this book as a tool, not just another bundle of paper on a shelf. If I ever meet you with this book after you've owned it for a while, I hope it's dog-eared and highlighted, with post-it notes sticking out all over. That's how the books look that have helped me the most.

Let's Get Started

In our time together, you'll discover that the ideas I offer will either be new to you or remind you of what you already know but perhaps aren't pursuing. You'll see that the shift from the Age of the Seller to the Age of the Customer is impacting every industry differently, but every organization significantly.

You'll find some level of execution detail—the how—in this book, but my primary goal is to encourage you to focus on what and why: what's changing and why it's happening. As the CEO of your organization, your mission is to develop strategies that will help your team execute the conversion of Age of the Customer disruptions into opportunities that will help you sustain success.

This book is designed to help you deliver on that mission. Now let's get started.

SECTION I

THIS HAS NEVER HAPPENED BEFORE

I like the dreams of the future better than the history of the past.

—Thomas Jefferson

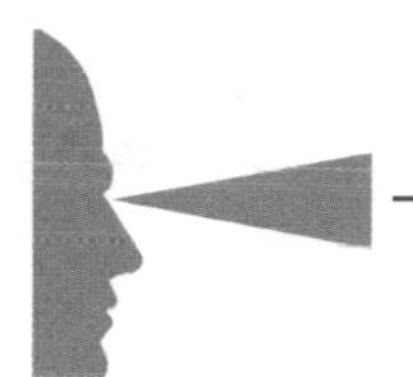

Section I

This Has Never Happened Before

Throughout this book, especially in this first section, you're going to see me refer to the concepts of a *paradigm*, a *paradigm shift*, and sometimes just *shift*. They're related, but different. The word *paradigm*, from the Greek, means "a pattern" or "example."

My introduction to the impact of paradigms came from futurist Joel Barker. Many years before Joel became a futurist expert on my radio program, his common-sense, plain-language approach to the power of paradigms changed how I looked at the world, which helped me envision the dynamic forces at work in the marketplace today and relate them to you here.

In his book, *Paradigms: The Business of Discovering the Future*, Barker aggregates the perspectives of other thinkers by describing a paradigm as the way we perceive the world—how our own paradigms have "explained the world to us." In *Powers of the Mind*, psychologist Adam Smith said paradigms are "a shared set of assumptions," and that when we're committed to a paradigm, "it's difficult to imagine any other paradigm." Paraphrasing Willis Harman, from *An Incomplete Guide to the Future*, a dominant paradigm exists unquestioned and is transmitted to succeeding generations "by direct experience, without being taught." As you'll see, the Age of the Seller is—was—a dominant paradigm.

But for all of his appropriate homage to other thinkers, I think Barker's own definition of a paradigm is the most useful: "A paradigm is a set of rules and regulations that: 1) establishes or defines boundaries, and 2) tells you how to behave inside those boundaries in order to be successful." And these rules, Barker says, can be written or unwritten.

Have You Ever Seen a Paradigm?

So what does a paradigm look like? An everyday, unwritten paradigm might be the unquestioned rules your parents established for the family. Games, like golf or chess, for example, are paradigms where the rules are written. Certainly an organized religion qualifies as a paradigm.

Remember, if you stay within the boundaries as you hang out with other subscribers to a paradigm, you're allowed to participate and pursue success. But if you don't play by the rules, you'll experience pressure from the paradigm police. Or worse, you might become the paradigm police.

Barker points out that, once established, paradigms are useful, because we find ways to be successful as we operate within their boundaries. For thousands of years, the Age of the Seller was a dominant paradigm that was so useful it provided humans with an economic foundation that literally funded the rise of civilization as we know it.

But there comes a time when any particular paradigm, even a dominant one that has been beneficial to you, actually becomes a problem—even dangerous. And when that time occurs, that's when a paradigm shift is likely to happen.

Barker says a paradigm shift is "when everything goes back to zero." When the rules, boundaries, practices, levers, and assumptions you've counted on for some period of time are now compromised, no longer viable, or perhaps even no longer available. A shift can happen over many years, but it can also happen overnight.

Here are two examples of shifts of dominant paradigms: Martin Luther's *Ninety-Five Theses* in 1517 is said to have been the origin of Protestantism, a historic paradigm shift for the established Catholic Church. The American Revolution, officially declared in 1776, produced a paradigm shift for the empire upon which it was said the sun never set.

Both of these shifts took years to unfold but fundamentally changed the rules and boundaries of both Christianity and British colonialism. In their respective paradigm shifts, Pope Leo X and King George III were both introduced to the sometimes rude wisdom of Ecclesiastes chapter 3, which at once promises that there is a time for everything, while warning that change is ordained, since nothing lasts forever.

Section I reveals a paradigm shift on a historic level of magnitude. This shift disrupts an entrenched, dominant paradigm that's older than the concepts of colonialism and organized religion—the original balance of power between Sellers and Customers.

It's ironic that Barker's work was so successful in re-introducing a new generation to the power of understanding the influence of paradigms that it became an oft-overused and misused buzz word. But a powerful word is never a cliché when employed as a compelling communication tool, like I'm going to do now: At this moment we're in the middle of a historic shift from one dominant paradigm to a new one. In the history of the marketplace, this has never happened before.

The purpose of the first section of this book is to reveal and define this shift and help you navigate it successfully.

The End of a Dominant Paradigm

There are very few opportunities for people living in the 21st century to say they were alive when something happened that had never happened before in the history of mankind and may never happen again. Yet this is what we're witnessing. The original marketplace Age is succumbing to a new Age. The Age of the Seller is coming to an end and the Age of the Customer is emerging. This conversion began at a very specific time, 1993, and will end at a less specific time.

The Age of the Seller has been in force since the origin of markets approximately 10,000 years ago, as humans became less nomadic and slowly started staying more or less in one place due to the domestication of animals and cultivation of crops. It is this original marketplace Age that is now seeing its last days.

As will be revealed, the foundational element common to both Ages is control of what arguably has become the most important and powerful asset—information. The transfer of access to and control of information in the marketplace is so unprecedented, and on such an order of magnitude, that I use a geologic metaphor to describe it. Furthermore, because of the compression of the lifespan of model generations caused by the velocity of this change, never before have the moments of opportunity and disruption been so near to each other that they give new meaning to the two-sided sword metaphor.

The tendency to either deny or fail to appreciate the magnitude of what is happening is reasonable to expect. Dominant paradigms die hard. But it must be understood that the shift to the Age of the Customer is happening, and your business is and will be influenced significantly.

Customers are making the shift from the old Age to the new without effort and often without even being conscious of it. But it's more difficult for Sellers, because their conversion can only occur when they accept that the marketplace they've always known is coming to an end, and make conscious and specific efforts to adjust to the new Age.

In Section I, I'm going to:

- allow you one last, quick look at the original paradigm, the Age of the Seller
- explain why the shift to the new paradigm, the Age of the Customer, is happening
- show how an era of parallel universes currently exists, but is waning
- reveal why and how changes in customer behavior is impacting your world
- introduce a single moment that can become either an opportunity or a disruption
- remind you of old Influencers and introduce two new ones
- reveal the power of adding a single letter to a classic marketplace standard
- make you happy to see that the best business practice of all time is only increasing in value

If you do nothing else that I recommend in this book, please commit the time to read, believe, and adopt the elements of Section I as your new understanding of how the marketplace works, today and in the future.

I'm convinced our future success in business—yours and mine—will depend upon such a commitment.

Chapter 1

The Age of the Seller

Markets were born when humans chose to acquire what they needed by trading with each other rather than producing it themselves or taking from someone else by theft or force.

The moment of conception for proto-market was when the first individual, the Seller, offered to trade with another, the Customer, and that offer was accepted.

And so it was for millennia; this marketplace dance was as beautifully simple as it was exquisitely effective, having at its nucleus three primary relationship elements:

1. The product, controlled by the Seller.
2. Information about the product, also controlled by the Seller.
3. The buying decision, controlled by the Customer.

Figure 1 demonstrates this control dynamic.

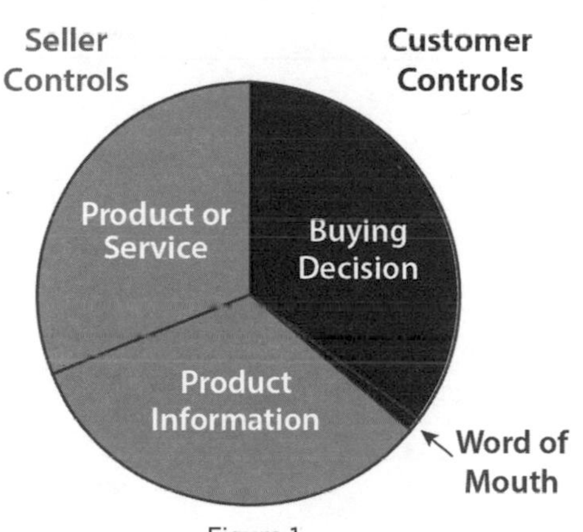

Figure 1
Primary Relationship Elements

From that first transaction when shells were the reserve currency, to a time very near to the end of the 20th century, the dance between a Seller and a Customer was performed zillions of times with little variation. I've termed this period the Age of the Seller. The logic is simply based on the 2:1 ratio of control, as depicted in Figure 1.

In the Age of the Seller, most of what the Customer needed to know about the product being offered—selection, application, availability, price, industry news, customer experience, etc.—was created, distributed, and controlled by the Seller. Indeed, for most of my career in sales, like a gazillion other sales professionals for thousands of years, I served as my Customer's primary information source for the things I sold. They looked to me to provide product information, help with applications, what I knew about customer experiences, industry news, maybe even an appraisal of the competitive landscape, and of course, availability and pricing.

Then something happened that accomplished what no other event or innovation had been able to do for 10 millennia—not the printing press, not the telephone, not radio, not television, not even smarter, more informed salespeople.

The birth of a new Age.

Chapter 2

The Age of the Customer

For the first time in 10,000 years, a new marketplace Age is born.

The birth of the Age of the Customer happened around April 30, 1993, when access to the Internet became commercially available to the general public. At that time, the Web browser Mosaic was introduced, which helped the average person take advantage of the World Wide Web. The creation, convergence, and adoption of the following innovations proved to be the beginning of the end of the Age of the Seller and the advent of the Age of the Customer:

- The personal computer
- Public availability of the Internet, infrastructure, and associated tools and applications, such as browsers, email, instant messaging, etc.
- Availability and saturation of high-speed Internet connections for both businesses and consumers
- Web 2.0—beyond passive viewing of websites, allowing interaction, sharing, and collaboration online
- Ubiquity of mobile computing—WiFi, mobile networks, etc.
- Global growth in high-functioning wireless devices, including laptops, smartphones, tablets, etc.

The millennia-old marketplace dance is still beautifully simple, but the Age of the Customer created a shift in who leads when the two dancers come together. Now here's the new paradigm:

- The buying decision is still controlled by the Customer.
- Products and services are still controlled by the Seller.
- Access to information, including customer experience, is now controlled by the Customer.

As you can see in Figure 2, the elements have shifted in terms of influence on control of the relationship, as Customer control waxes and Seller control wanes.

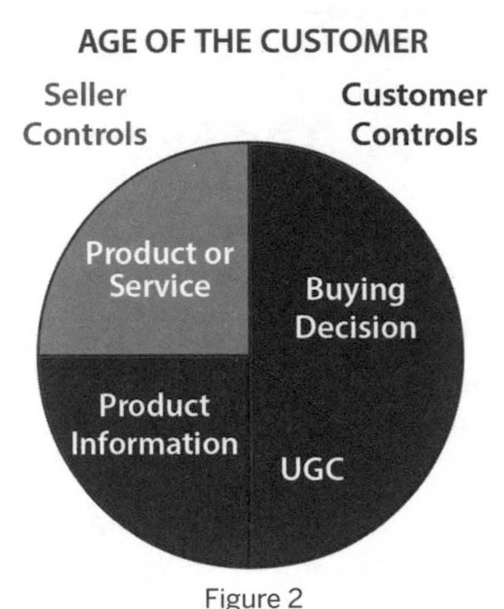

Figure 2
Primary Relationship Elements

You'll notice that the small sliver in the Age of the Seller chart, identified as Word of Mouth in Figure 1, has grown in the Age of the Customer and has a new name: User Generated Content, or UGC. UGC is a powerful element of the new Age, which we'll discuss later in more detail.

Let's take a look at how and why this shift is impacting these elements.

The Product

In the new Age, control of the Product or Service element still remains with the Seller, but has diminished as a control factor. This is because:

- Virtually everything a business can sell has become a commodity, which is to say, readily available from multiple sources at a comparable price.
- It's much less frequent for a Seller to introduce an innovation that is so unique that it provides any level of control over Customers. With a few exceptions, the "killer app" phenomenon has seen better days.
- For millennia, customer purchase options were from a limited number of merchants. In the new Age, Customers have multiple shopping and purchasing options, including traditional brick-and-mortar Sellers and a seemingly infinite array of online Sellers.

The Buying Decision

As it has always been, the Customer retains control of the buying decision in the new Age. The only change is that this control element has shifted even more in favor of the Customer, primarily due to shifts in the next element—information. And as you'll see in chapter 5, "The Moment of Relevance," the shift in the buying decision process in the Age of the Customer will at once produce opportunity and disruption.

The Information

Perhaps not since the coincidental convergence of the Protestant Reformation and Gutenberg's Bible has there been such a historic shift of knowledge and control; indeed, a perfect storm of innovations has made the following possible:

- The entire universe of human knowledge—including information formerly controlled by Sellers—is now generally available to the entire universe of humans with a very low barrier-to-entry.
- Humans now have the ability to discover, learn, comment on, and share their experiences, opinions, and appraisals.

Word of Mouth

In the Age of the Seller, the distribution of customer experiences was primarily a function of the word-of-mouth phenomenon, which historically was incidental and had a marginal impact on how a Seller conducted business. There's an old marketplace maxim that goes: "If a customer likes you, they will tell someone, but if they don't like you, they will tell 10 people."

> **THIS WILL BE ON THE TEST**
>
> *UGC is word of mouth on steroids.*

The impact of this word-of-mouth ratio on how Sellers behaved diminished as a business grew larger. Practically speaking, a Main Street small business with a smaller customer base was more negatively impacted by the 1:10 ratio than was a major corporation, which likely possessed an intimidating brand supported by a significant marketing budget.

In the new Age, the influence of the customer experience has expanded and morphed from traditional word of mouth into the dynamic and very compelling phenomenon, UGC. Essentially online word of mouth, UGC is the posting on digital platforms of experiences, attitudes, questions, praise, or condemnation of a Seller's products and services. As one of the key markers of Web 2.0, UGC has several variations. But for our purposes, I'm going to use UGC throughout this book as a handy term to refer to any digital commenting about a Seller by someone who's outside, like a Customer.

Traditional word of mouth is not going away. But UGC is word of mouth on steroids; it is, and will continue to be, a very powerful force in the new Age. The same technological innovations and applications that are making it easier for Sellers to publish content and brand messages has also produced the tools and platforms that allow Customers to write, record, video, and then publish and distribute their experiences with a Seller, plus a general opinion of a Seller's behavior in the marketplace.

Today, the word-of-mouth maxim sounds more like this:

Whether Customers like you or not, they have the ability to potentially tell millions.

The incidence and consequence of commenting by Customers from word of mouth to UGC is, as Mark Twain said, like the difference between a lightning bug and lightning. Consequently, in the Age of the Customer, there is no place for a Seller—or their behavior—to hide.

A Picture Is Worth a Thousand Words

Here's the side-by-side comparison that demonstrates the dramatic shift in control:

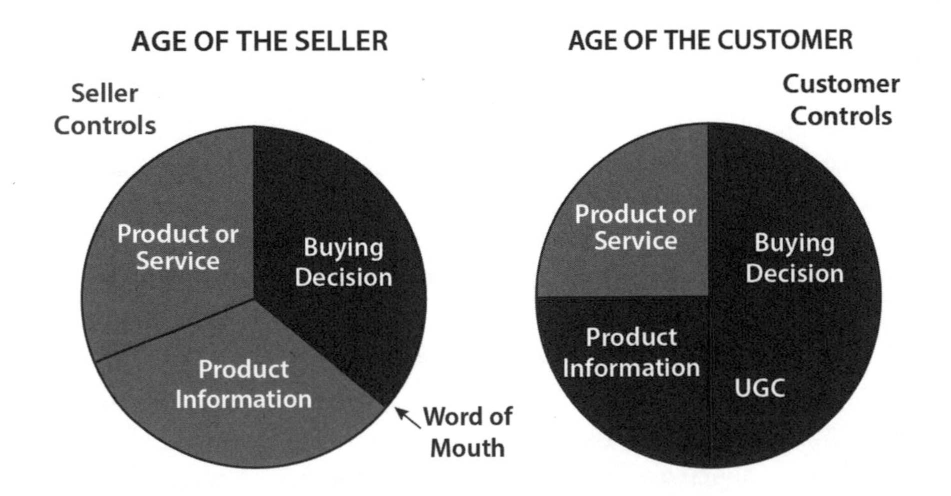

Upon seeing how diminished your control as a Seller is becoming in the new Age, don't be alarmed if you start feeling sweat on your forehead or get heart palpitations. That just means you're starting to realize why your marketing, advertising, and sales efforts aren't creating the performance they once did. To paraphrase author Spencer Johnson, the Age of the Customer is moving your cheese.

But fear not. That's what this book is for—to replace those negative responses with understanding about what's happening, why it's happening, and how you can profit from the shift, instead of being run over by it.

I'm glad you're here. We're going to have fun.

The new source of power is not money in the hands of a few, but information in the hands of many.

—John Naisbitt

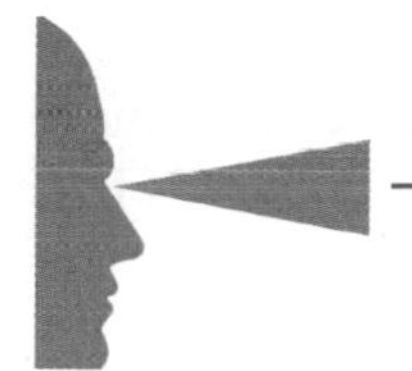

Chapter 3

Parallel Universes

Compared to the historical timeline and pace of marketplace evolution, the shift to the Age of the Customer is happening at light speed. Nevertheless, since the Age of the Seller was the original standard by which markets were born and flourished for thousands of years, complete conversion will take time. Consequently, the two Ages now exist as parallel universes and will do so until the old Age finally succumbs to the new one.

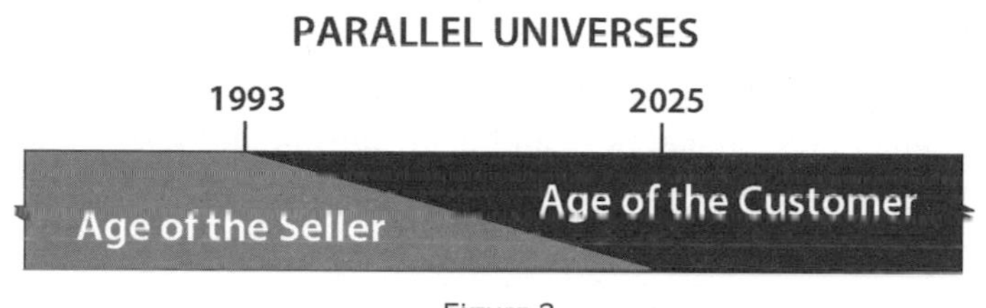

Figure 3

As you can see in Figure 3, I'm projecting that the parallel universes will span approximately 30 years, because ...

- As previously shown, the beginning of the Age of the Customer was 1993, the year commercial use of the Internet was first allowed.
- The year 2025 is my estimate for the end of the Age of the Seller because:
    - The Age of the Customer 2:1 control ratio should be fully diffused across all customer demographics and communities by then.
    - The last vestiges of Sellers resisting the new control ratio will be extinct, having exhausted their equity and/or credit availability by then.

The conversion timeline from the old Age to the new will be different for every industry, just as conversion for business-to-consumer retailers will differ from the business-to-business sector. The conversion landscape will be populated by two categories of Sellers: Visionary and Hidebound.

Visionary Sellers

These businesses are converting their growth and capitalization plans to conform to the new Age reality of more Customer control. Visionary Sellers can be identified by these markers:

- They encourage and respond quickly to customer communication and interaction, regardless of how granular it may be.
- They organize to quickly respond to customer experience feedback.
- They train their sales force to recognize and serve the increasingly informed, prepared, decisive, and empowered Customer.
- They recognize that the increased sunlight of the new Age requires strategies and brand messaging to align with actual c7ustomer experiences likely documented and published as UGC.
- They're always working to track and respond to rapidly changing customer expectations.

The default marketing strategy of Visionary Sellers will be focused more on authenticity, connection, and contribution and less on solicitation, manipulation, and puffery.

Here's a true story that's a great example of visionary behavior:

With its origins traced back to 1911, International Business Machines became one of the most dominant companies in the world. Leading the technology sector, IBM computer hardware and software were considered the gold standard for most of the 20th century.

But nothing lasts forever. After the company lost $8 billion in 1993, the largest ever at that time by any corporation, IBM was in peril of not surviving. That's when IBM leadership, under the command of CEO Louis Gerstner, made the visionary acknowledgement that IBM could no longer focus only on hardware and software; they would dilute dependence on those products by expanding their portfolio to include services.

While truly gut-wrenching for the octogenarian IBM culture, what resulted from the recognition that the future does not fit in the container of the past was one of the most dramatic turnarounds in corporate history.

→

As of this writing, services account for half of IBM revenues. The vision of this decision was in seeing that the future of hardware and software was toward commoditization, but the future of services was toward customization. Commodities are traded at the lowest margin of all offerings. Services, especially those that are customized, are among the highest gross profit margin products.

Today, IBM is one of the top U.S. companies in most critical categories. But without visionary leadership, it might have been little more than a footnote in corporate history.

Hidebound Sellers

These are Sellers whose investment in the old order of control is so embedded and inbred that they continue to deny the reality in front of them. These Sellers can be identified by the following markers:

- Misplaced frustration: As is often the case when Sellers begin to feel the influence of any disruptive shift, the frustration of those heavily invested in the waning paradigm think their pain is caused by a failure to execute.
- Bad decisions: It is said that armies prepare for the future by training for the last war. So it is with Hidebound Sellers. Not only do Age of the Customer forces make them think they're being attacked, but they persist in using obsolete Age of the Seller countermeasures.
- Destructive pressure: Convinced of execution failure, pressure brought to bear on the organization by management results in an employee casualty list instead of a growing and strengthening customer list.
- Equity erosion: Defiance in the face of overwhelming evidence will sustain the deniers until they run out of Customers who have not yet empowered themselves with the leverage of the new Age or their equity and access to credit is depleted.

Here's another true story that is a classic example of hidebound behavior:

A national retailer with hundreds of stores was losing market share. Instead of working on the things that would actually focus on the new and evolving expectations of their customers, management decided that the solution to their problem was to create a new marketing campaign, complete with a new slogan. They even tested the slogan with focus groups, and, incredibly, in the announcement of the new campaign, the quoted executive actually talked about how appealing this new slogan was to their test audience. Here is a portion of the actual press release to announce the new strategy:

"As part of a larger campaign to include a new look, feel, and image, both internally and externally, the marketing strategy also includes a new tagline and advertising campaign that reflects our unwavering commitment to customers.

"Television and radio ads are to focus on the idea of [XYZ Company] as the partner customers depend on to provide essential tools to get the job done right. The new tagline communicates a clear and meaningful message to customers. Further, it shows our desire to take on the competition ... and win!"

Keep in mind that this was not an internal communication; it was released to the press and the public. There was nothing about what the company was actually going to do to serve Customers better, only that they had a new "look, feel, and image" and a new "tagline," and that Customers would get the idea of their new "meaningful message." Also, notice the proud reference to taking on the competition, as if that matters to Customers.

Incidentally, the industry in which this company operates conducted a customer survey prior to this press release, where shoppers leaving stores of the industry's three major players were asked if they could say the name of the store they had just been in. Six out of ten respondents could not do so correctly, even though each competitor had distinctive marketing campaigns and slogans.

Extinction Is Avoidable

Hidebound Sellers are the dinosaurs of the Quaternary Period. And like their unfortunate Jurassic namesakes, they're becoming extinct as marketplace natural selection subjects them to the slow, painful, and expensive death of irrelevance. But unlike those that took place millions of years ago, extinctions caused by the Age of the Customer are preventable.

At this moment, most Sellers have one foot on the Age of the Seller dock and one in the Age of the Customer boat, which is moving away from the dock. First, you must commit to eliminate any vestiges of being hidebound and shift toward visionary behavior. By making this commitment, you'll not only be better able to fully commit all aspects of your business to Age of the Customer practices, but your organization will also be prepared to make the shift without creating a casualty list.

THIS WILL BE ON THE TEST

Hidebound Sellers—large and small—are the dinosaurs of the Quaternary Period.

All of this activity is happening now for all businesses and at different paces for each industry. But it is happening fast for everyone, and stepping from the dock to the boat will be required sooner than later. You don't have any time to waste.

Life is largely a matter of expectation.

—Horace

Chapter 4

Subduction of Expectations

Many historical and classic examples exist of products and industries that have experienced disruptions by an innovation. Consider the following, listed with their disrupters in parentheses: swords (gunpowder), buggy whips (autos), transcontinental passenger trains (airplanes), slide rules (calculators), CDs (iPod), fax machines (email), personal computers (smartphones), etc.

Of course, you can still buy all of these things and some people still use them. But their usage is now essentially relegated to novelty status, and unless you're in the novelty business, that's not a sustainable business model.

In my own career, I worked for Xerox at a time when you couldn't purchase their plain paper copiers outright, you could only rent them. In fact, for decades Xerox's entire business model was built around this rental strategy, as it was for all of their U.S. plain paper copier competitors.

This model worked fine for Xerox until about 1977. That's when Japanese copier companies, for example, Savin, introduced plain paper copiers to the U.S. market that you could either rent or buy. And when purchased with the available financing, this plain paper option usually resulted in a lower monthly cost. In less than three years, millions of small businesses now had new expectations regarding the acquisition of plain paper copiers.

By the time Xerox realized they had to conform to the new customer expectations about acquiring a copier and respond with their own purchase/finance option, they had lost market share at a breathtaking rate. Frankly, the company barely survived and was never the same after that.

Now let's take that truth beyond the product and industry application and apply it to the entire marketplace.

The Power of Subduction

In the previous chapter, the parallel universe analogy and graphic depicts the chronology of the shift from the Age of the Seller to the Age of the

Customer, but not the dynamism and disruptiveness. The best way to think about the movement, energy, and pressure that the new Age is imposing on the old one is with a geological analogy, specifically the shifting of tectonic plates.

When two tectonic plates of Earth's crust collide, since both can't occupy the same space, something has to give. That something is called subduction, as one of the plates overrides and subducts the other. Figure 4 depicts what the subduction of the old Age by the new would look like if they were colliding tectonic plates.

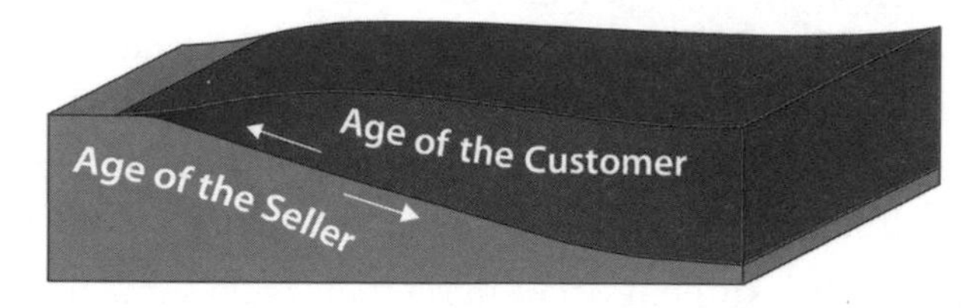

Figure 4

In a later chapters, I'll spend more time explaining how specific Age of the Seller elements are being overridden by Age of the Customer elements, plus one completely new element that has no marketplace comparable in the original Age. For now, we'll use the subduction theme to demonstrate how Age of the Seller customer expectations are succumbing to customer expectations in the new Age.

BLASINGAME'S LAW OF CUSTOMER EXPECTATIONS

Once a new capability or advantage is available to Customers and adopted, that becomes their new minimum expectation.

The Subduction of Expectations

As stated in the previous chapter, the subduction zone spans approximately 30 years, during which the new Age will override the original one. The following illustrations dramatically demonstrate the evolution of customer expectations as the Age of the Customer subducts the Age of the Seller. As you can see in Figure 5, prior to 2008 many Sellers could operate reasonably well with Age of the Seller practices, because there wasn't much pressure from new Age expectations.

But Figure 6 clearly shows why many Sellers are confused and frustrated, especially the hidebound ones mentioned in chapter 3. They don't understand why they're running out of Prospects and Customers whose expectations can be fulfilled with Age of the Seller solutions.

The vertical lines in the middle of these two graphs indicate an increase in the velocity of the subduction around 2008. This new trajectory is based on my estimate that a significant increase in the adoption rate of social media and mobile computing began around that time.

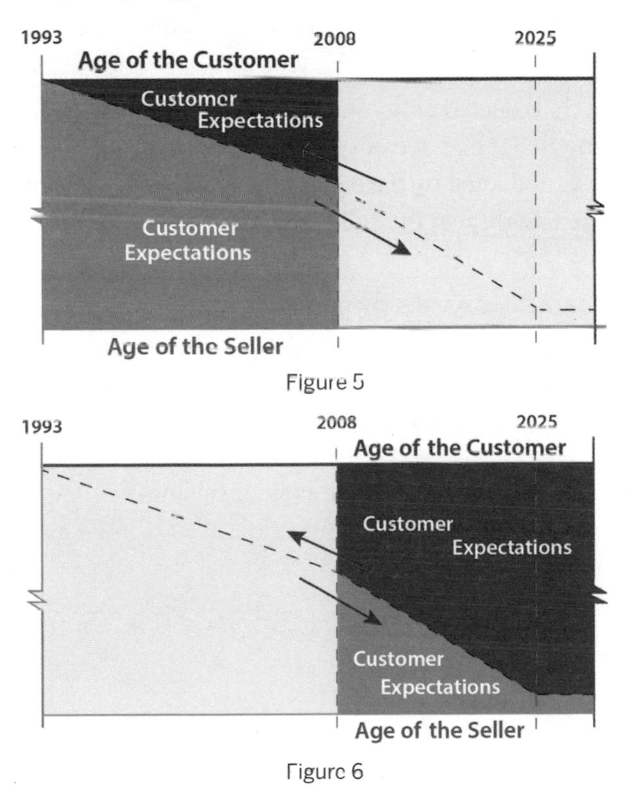

Figure 5

Figure 6

Please take this profound quote to heart:

The future does not fit into the container of the past.

—Rishad Tobaccowala
Chief Strategy & Innovation Officer, VivaKi

The social media phenomenon has many markers, but one that is closely associated with the Age of the Customer is the information-sharing that takes place in the millions of new personal and business online communities created by social media activity. And the more online communities flourish and share, the more Customers are empowered with new expectations.

Which Tectonic Plate Are You On?

Any level of discomfort—frustration, fear, anxiety, etc.—you may feel as you look at the subduction dynamic happening on the right side of Figure 6 will be in direct proportion to how committed you are to Age of the Seller practices. And as you can see, time is not on the side of your discomfort.

In geology, a subducted entity isn't necessarily termed the loser. But in the marketplace, any Seller that doesn't make appropriate and timely adjustments to prevent being subducted by the Age of the Customer will not only become a loser, but increasingly feel the full force of:

BLASINGAME'S PRIME MARKETPLACE LAW

The marketplace is indifferent to your very existence, let alone your survival and success.

Which marketplace tectonic plate is your business riding on? Tick-tock.

Chapter 5

The Moment of Relevance

As revealed in chapter 1, one of the three major elements of the relationship between Sellers and Customers is the buying decision. And even though control of this element hasn't changed in 10,000 years, how the buying decision is made in the Age of the Customer, including the tools used by Customers, has changed dramatically.

In the Age of the Seller, the way Customers selected prospective Sellers included: being exposed to marketing messages and advertised offerings; shopping in the Seller's physical location; being called on by a salesperson; word of mouth; and, ultimately, direct mail, catalogs, and telephone. As this process played out zillions of times over the millennia, the Customer would regularly be required to contact a Seller to get the information needed to complete the selection process and make a purchase. Consequently, one of the advantages in the Age of the Seller was the high likelihood that a Seller would have direct access to and potential influence on Customers as they were making their buying decision and before they made a purchase.

Today, the need for a Customer to narrow the seemingly endless field of potential Sellers is more important than ever. But that elemental Seller advantage—access to Customers—has been disrupted by Age of the Customer innovations. And as you will learn, in some cases that disruption happens literally at the moment it takes to twitch an index finger.

The Prefix That Changed the World

One of my Brain Trust members is Anita Rosen. Anita was on one of the early pioneering teams that shaped the experience of Internet users in the mid-90s, and we're all fortunate that she has continued her thought leadership of the online universe. In a 2003 interview with me, Anita explained the concept of e-business and said to think of it as an umbrella under which there are three primary components: e-commerce, e-shopping, and e-customer service.

Of course, all three of these terms are intuitive—merely the electronic version of age-old marketplace behaviors. But perhaps no prefix in history has ever wielded as much potential to change the world as does the lowly "e." Innovations that gave rise to prefixing "e" to business, commerce, shopping, and customer service added new meaning to another "e" word: empower. In an unprecedented way, e-business elements have empowered those who now drive the economies on planet Earth—Customers. And it's this empowerment that has so dramatically changed the marketplace and the world.

BLASINGAME'S LAW OF CUSTOMER EMPOWERMENT

When Customers are empowered, Sellers are disrupted.

The Empowerment

In the Age of the Customer, the empowerment/disruption dynamic is happening at what I have named the Moment of Relevance.

The Internet and associated applications have made the entire universe of human knowledge available to the entire universe of humans with a very low barrier to entry. In the Age of the Customer, these new developments have converged to:

- Empower Customers with access to a global universe of Sellers—both traditional and online—plus the ability to compare offerings and educate themselves about anticipated purchases. This information empowerment has also created new pressure on Customers to find a quicker way to rule Sellers in or out.
- Empower Customers with new and innovative appraisal tools that are rendering the traditional Seller's access advantage irrelevant and obsolete.

The Disruption

Increasingly, the process of elimination of Sellers is taking place online, without the Customer having to make direct contact with a Seller. This direct contact disruption is doing more to change the dynamic of competition than anything in the history of the marketplace.

In the Age of the Customer, Sellers still have to be competitive with product, selection, service, and price. But while being competitive was the coin of the realm for thousands of years, today it's merely table stakes.

In the new Age, the greatest danger for every business is not being uncompetitive, but becoming irrelevant. And a Seller's success or failure at avoiding that peril happens at the Moment of Relevance.

At the Moment of Relevance, which occurs primarily in the virtual marketplace, two things happen that are extremely disruptive to any business still invested in Age of the Seller practices:

- Existing Customers have access to virtually all the information they need before the Seller even knows they're interested;
- Prospects are similarly informed before the Seller even knows they exist.

THIS WILL BE ON THE TEST

The greatest danger in the new Age is not being uncompetitive, but becoming irrelevant.

With the world of information at their fingertips, an almost infinite number of choices and the increasing influence of UGC, achieving the first step in a Customer's due diligence—who's competitive and who isn't—doesn't take very long. Indeed, many online resources rank companies by all of the classic competitive elements: price, selection, service, availability, etc.

But evolving customer expectations in the new Age have raised the selection bar above mere competitiveness to the point where relevance is becoming the ultimate standard of Seller performance.

BLASINGAME'S LAW OF RELEVANCE

In the Age of the Customer, relevance trumps competitiveness.

Relevance vs. Service

How is relevance different from service? By definition, service required some effort by the Seller. But today, Prospects and Customers have the ability to help themselves, in many cases online, in every step from shopping to buying to taking delivery. Anything a Customer can do for themselves is where service stops and relevance begins.

The Expectation of Relevance

A few, but certainly not all, examples of Age of the Customer expectations that come into play at the Moment of Relevance include:

- Does the Seller have a website?
- Is the website optimized for local search?
- Is the website easy to navigate?
- Does the Seller have a mobile site?
- Is the phone number easy to find and "hot" so mobile visitors can click to call?
- Are there directions to the physical location?
- Is e-commerce possible, where applicable?
- Are there comprehensive e-commerce credit/debit options?
- Are Customer reviews available or possible?
- Is there online support?
- Are there multiple options for visitors to give the Seller permission to follow-up digitally?
- (Your relevance preference here.)

Over time, this list will evolve based on emerging technologies and adoption rates, plus it will expand based on individual Customer preferences.

In chapter 4, I used a geological metaphor to demonstrate how the Age of the Seller is being subducted by the Age of the Customer. If you want to observe the moving, leading edge of this collision as the new Age overrides the old one, watch the evolution and expansion of Moment of Relevance expectations.

Moment of Relevance Stories

Here's how one company brought their business model, which is as Age of the Seller as it gets—selling groceries—into the new Age by adding relevance components. The result was that they not only beat the competition, but made more money in the process.

Some of the components of relevance are: helping Customers do something for themselves, technology, online, mobile, time saving, etc. Take a look at some of the relevance factors for this grocery store giant.

- From the company's website, grocery shoppers can create a shopping list from the current ad, as well as add other items. When they select the items they want to buy, the location of the items in the store is shown.
- The shopping list can be printed or emailed to a mobile device for use in the store.
- There's an app that presents current ads for the local store, including online coupons and special offers.
- Predictive staffing software helps the company have enough employees ready to keep checkout lines moving.

Here are the customer relevance factors in this list: planning, save money, save time, paperless, mobile, all of this using the tools and technology more and more grocery shoppers have.

> **THIS WILL BE ON THE TEST**
>
> *Anything a Customer can do for themselves is where service stops and relevance begins.*

Notice there was no mention of this company being cheaper than their competitors. On the contrary, other than sale items from week to week, customers aren't devoted because of price, they're devoted because of the entirety of the relevance factors, but also the cost of groceries is not out of line.

Now, here's the payoff for the company: It's common knowledge that grocery Sellers are doing great if they have a 2% net margin with 3% being an operating home run. But this company, Publix, averages over 5% net margin. How do they exceed industry levels? They've identified what is relevant to grocery shoppers and they deliver that—and charge for it.

Here's what Publix president Todd Jones said about their strategy. "We believe there are three ways to differentiate: service, quality, and price. You've got to be good at two of them, and the best at one. We make service our number one, then quality and then price."

Mr. Jones is talking about service first, but he's using Age of the Customer resources to help customers help themselves using their tools. That's part of the definition of relevance. And here's the big lesson for small businesses: He's not fighting the price war. He's charging enough to get the profit margins he wants, knowing that there are enough people out there who will pay his price for this level of relevance.

This model is how every small business should think about doing business in the Age of the Customer.

Two simple stories demonstrate how relevance can trump competitiveness in the new Age.

Reservation Peace of Mind

An executive is traveling to meet with customers in their city. As she checks in late at the hotel, she realizes she didn't make reservations for a lunch meeting the next day. She is aware of three restaurants in the area and has a preference, but it's 11:00 p.m. and, before she goes to bed, she needs to know that she has a place reserved to take her customers to lunch tomorrow.

Opening her laptop, she searches for her preferred restaurant and finds that it doesn't have a website, just a listing in "Area Restaurants." Even though a phone number is listed, it's now after closing time.

Her next search finds that the other two restaurants both have websites, but only one has after-hours reservations capability. Even though the latter restaurant would not have been competitive by Age of the Seller standards—higher prices, limited menu, and not as convenient—it is more relevant to this customer because it's available 24/7/365. Consequently, relevance trumped competitiveness and they got the business.

A Part in Time

A business owner and his team are working late to meet a customer deadline by noon the next day. When a part breaks, they have to stop for the night, but before the owner leaves the office, he needs to find where he can buy a replacement part and get it to his shop early the next morning.

He finds the websites of the two local parts suppliers, but only one has a parts catalog listed. And not only does the website show that this supplier offers the part needed, but also that they have units in stock.

The price for the part is listed, but our business owner doesn't look at it, because at this point he only wants to know where to have an employee sitting when that business opens the next morning. Relevance trumps competitiveness—again.

Prepare for the Moment of Relevance

Any Seller who wants to have the maximum opportunity to survive and thrive in the Age of the Customer will become an expert on how the Moment of Relevance is becoming the new coin of the realm.

What are you doing to put yourself in position to be no more than one level of expectation behind the latest and greatest? I think Customers who know and like you won't require you to push the envelope with leading edge relevance innovations. But they won't stay with you for long if you fall behind.

Remember, relevance is a mercurial and finicky thing. Knowing how well you're moving the needle on your Customers' relevance meter will require constant close contact with them. And you'll have to think of this level of customer engagement as a way of life, not just a means to an end.

As digital capability becomes more micro simultaneous with being more mobile, Customers are acquiring new relevance expectations every day. And they're increasingly expecting whoever they do business with to meet those expectations at the Moment of Relevance.

The humblest individual exerts some influence, either for good or bad, upon others.

—Henry Ward Beecher

Chapter 6

The Influencers

The face-to-face aspect of the relationship between Sellers and Customers has been forged over millennia. Even the advent of written correspondence and first-generation electronic communication, like the telephone, didn't significantly alter the compelling face-to-face dynamic between the two partners in the marketplace dance.

In the Age of the Seller, face-to-face also had an impact on how Customers influenced others about a Seller's performance through word of mouth. First, they had to literally come into contact to create an experience, which primarily involved a face-to-face meeting. Plus the process of influencing others about their experience with a Seller was also typically associated with a one-on-one engagement.

In the original Age, face-to-face worked to the advantage of the Seller. But as we discuss the new kinds of Influencers, you'll notice how elements of the Age of the Customer have diminished a Seller's face-to-face advantage and, as in other examples, that advantage has been transferred to the Customer.

The Original Influencers

In the Age of the Seller, three groups mattered to a business for sales growth: Suspects, Prospects, and Customers. Here's how a Seller met and interacted with these three, in order of appearance.

A Suspect is anybody and everybody. Think of the names in the local phone book (remember those?). Initially, a Seller had no relationship with a Suspect until contact was made in some way and the process of qualifying them began. A Suspect became a Prospect when they met a Seller's qualifying criteria and the relationship developed—usually face-to-face—until they were turned into a Customer, or not.

No Seller operates in an appraisal vacuum. Every interaction in the marketplace produces some kind of evaluation or appraisal opportunity that can be conveyed to others by the person on the receiving end of the interaction.

Let's call these potential appraisers Influencers. For 10,000 years, only Prospects and Customers were Influencers, because they had exposure and interaction with a Seller. Suspects were typically not Influencers.

In the Age of the Customer, Sellers are navigating a marketplace environment where online activity and behavior are constantly being appraised by more than just Prospects and Customers. Indeed, there are now four Influencers of your business, including the original two, Prospects and Customers, plus the new ones, Users and Communities.

A New Influencer: Users

Since Prospects and Customers already have a relationship with your business, it's likely they have some level of appraisal about you and the ability to influence others, whether through classic word of mouth or UGC.

The first new group, Users, have become Influencers just since the advent of the Age of the Customer. Like Suspects in the original Age, Users are people you probably have not yet developed a business relationship with. But Users are unlike Suspects in at least three very important ways:

1. With the Internet, Users can easily find you, your offerings, information, and online behavior and make an appraisal—good or not so much—without ever having met you or visited your business, which also means without you even knowing they exist.
2. Users have the potential to influence others by posting their appraisal on a Seller's customer comment platform and open UGC platforms, such as Yelp.com, Angieslist.com, etc.
3. Historically, Sellers have invested lots of money in mystery shopper consultants to penetrate their marketing and sales environment and report their experience to management. Users are the Age of the Customer version of mystery shoppers. The good news is they're essentially free. The bad news is their report doesn't go to management—it goes to the online universe.

But there are at least three ways to think of Users as a positive addition:

1. The very act of finding you, especially if they leave a UGC trail, means that they reveal themselves to you.
2. Some form of contact information (email, username, etc.) is likely disclosed due to the method of contact.

3. They have demonstrated at least a tacit interest in what you sell, which is essentially self-qualifying themselves without any direct cost or involvement by you.

Users are a new class of Suspects; think of them as Suspects on steroids. If you're wondering about the power of this new Influencer category, remember this: The drivers of value for the big social media platforms—Facebook, Twitter, LinkedIn, etc.—are Users, not Customers.

But just because you don't have the same business model as Facebook doesn't mean you can't find a way to benefit from the power of Users. And every small business has the ability to convert a User into a paying Customer in a way that makes Facebook, Twitter, and LinkedIn green with envy.

Every Seller must develop a strategy to turn Users into Prospects.

A New Influencer: Communities

Two of the most powerful developments of human existence are the concepts and reality of Community and market. Community is listed first intentionally because, before there were markets, there were Communities. Indeed, because humans are primordially gregarious, before we did business together, we congregated.

In the Age of the Seller, the concept of Community became associated with the development of society, while market was affixed to the development of business and trade. But in the Age of the Customer, the nomenclature of business has been expanded to include Community, and your business's future survival will depend upon your ability to understand this shift.

> **THIS WILL BE ON THE TEST**
>
> *Every small business has the ability to convert a User into a paying Customer.*

There is great advantage for a business to segment its market activity. We have customer lists, prospect development lists, suspect profile lists, etc. These are all Age of the Seller segments that have served us well, but all became a segment or list because of some direct action taken or connection made by a Seller with a Customer or Prospect.

Here's an Age of the Seller Community example that's a useful analogy. For many years, Sellers have used a Community prospecting strategy by building relationships with trade group memberships. Unfortunately for most Sellers, this was typically not the primary prospecting activity. Nevertheless, the trade group prospecting model is an excellent one to use to understand the benefits of developing relationships with online Communities because:

- The Community has to be found and the Seller has to participate.
- Increasingly members of these Communities will require Sellers to demonstrate their values by contributing to the Community in advance of any business opportunity. We'll talk more about this in chapter 7.

In the new Age, these classic segments will still produce Customers, but here's the shift: Increasingly, Prospects and Customers will be found through their association with activity in online Communities.

Three reasons why your segments and lists should now be referred to as Communities include:

1. More and more business activity is being influenced by the Internet. So it makes sense to start thinking of all marketplace activity in terms of Communities because of the connection opportunity. Customers on lists become members of customer Communities when they have the ability to interact among themselves.
2. As the table on the facing page shows, unlike lists, Communities aren't static; they're very dynamic. A Prospect on a list is an unconnected name, inert until a purchase is made. A Customer with access to the Community becomes potentially dynamic and engaged with endless influencing, connecting, and buying possibilities.
3. As your universe of Users, Prospects, and Customers gravitates toward the online world as part of their sense of Community, this movement will trump demographic behavior. This means that you may be more likely to reach a 55-year-old female in a Master Gardening Community than you are to reach her as a member of her age, education, or income demographic.

The principle of Community is timeless. As innovative platforms come and go, the primordial human need to connect with others remains, whether physically or virtually. In the Age of the Customer, Community is not prominent because it can be, but because we need it.

In the New Age, Community Will Trump Demographic

One thing that defines the new Age is that Customer behavior will be increasingly influenced by the dynamic values of the Communities they associate with and less by a predetermined demographic profile. In plain language, Community will increasingly trump generation, ethnicity, income, education, and gender.

In the Age of the Seller, using a demographic profile would get a Seller close enough to customer behavior to be reasonably successful. In the new Age, where technology allows Customers to more freely associate and communicate based on values and interests rather than demographic influences, success will require a more granular approach that recognizes the following comparison of Communities and demographics:

Communities vs. Demographics

DEMOGRAPHICS	COMMUNITIES
Demographics are inert.	Communities are dynamic.
Demographics don't communicate, they just exist.	Communities connect, interact and share.
A demographic essentially represents dated documents: birth certificate, diplomas, marriage license, financial statements, etc.	Communities are created, joined, and left by the members at will.
Demographics are large.	Communities can be any size.
Demographics don't change without some dramatic event.	Communities are dynamic and change frequently, both in membership and interests.
Demographic behavior is not dynamic.	Community behavior is influenced by relationships and experiences, both of which are constantly evolving.
Demographics create nothing.	Communities create and share information and experiences (UGC).
Demographics have no rules.	Communities are self-governing.
Demographics have no appraisal capacity.	Communities scrutinize and verify marketing messages.
Demographics are not based on values.	Communities place a high value on a Seller's demonstrated compatible values.

Prepare for the Moment of Relevance

There's an old law enforcement warning that can be applied to your relationship with all of the Influencers: You can run, but you can't hide.

As Sellers in the Age of the Customer, our constant commitment has to be to do whatever is necessary to be picked up on the digital and analog radar of Influencers. We have to do our best to make that image a positive one, whether we're being visited by a User, probed by a Prospect, appraised by a Community, or engaged by a Customer.

Many Sellers are not prepared to be scrutinized on such a comprehensive and intense scale. But the closer the Age of the Seller comes to being fully subducted and replaced by the new Age, being constantly and anonymously evaluated will be your reality. Start now identifying the ways your business is regarded by all Influencers, identify the weak points, and fix them.

Don't worry; the Influencers will tell you where you need to focus improvement. But they won't knock on your door or mail you this information. You have to stay close to your Influencers, listen, and believe what they're telling you about what is relevant to them.

In the Age of the Customer, the most dramatic difference between a demographic and a Community is the focus on values, which we'll discuss in the next chapter.

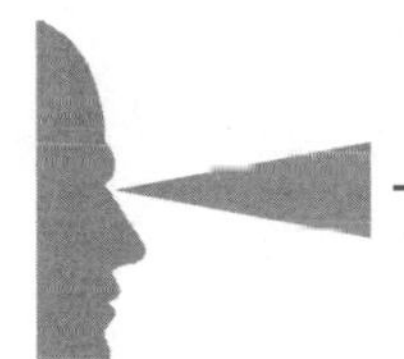

Chapter 7

Value and Values

Economic theory could be revolutionized by accepting the reality of human love for the highest values.

—Abraham Maslow, Psychologist
Creator of Maslow's Hierarchy of Needs

Receiving value, primarily associated with the classic array of price, product, service, customization, etc., was the prime customer expectation of the Age of the Seller. And how successful a Customer was in value received depended heavily on the competitive landscape. Nevertheless, no Customer ever wanted to spend more than they had to or settle for bad service. In the Age of the Customer, this hasn't changed.

What has changed in the new Age is the disruption of that competitive landscape. The forces of globalization and the Internet have resulted in virtually everything you sell becoming a commodity; even basic service has fallen into the commodity category. Since essentially everything a Customer could need or want is available so ubiquitously, Customers now presume that they will receive value in every transaction. Consequently, they're looking for new differentiators, which is what this chapter is about.

How a Hallmark Changed by Adding One Letter

Isn't it interesting how adding a single letter can turn the world upside down? In chapter 5, "The Moment of Relevance," you saw how simply prefixing an "e" in front of millennia-old marketplace concepts essentially changed the standard of marketplace viability—competitiveness. As you are about to see, suffixing a single letter to another marketplace imperative names a customer expectation increasingly more powerful than the root word.

In the Age of the Seller, value was the hallmark of competitiveness. In the Age of the Customer, where relevance is the new prime expectation, value, like competitiveness, is now merely table stakes.

With value now presumed, Customers are increasingly incorporating into their decision-making process an appraisal of a Seller that is expanded by one letter; they're taking into consideration not just value delivered, but also values demonstrated. How a Seller articulates, demonstrates, and delivers on those values—whether stated by the Seller or expected by Customers—is now very much a part of the relevance dynamic.

THIS WILL BE ON THE TEST

Customers now presume that they will receive value in every transaction.

With the addition of one letter, the hallmark question of the Age of the Seller, "Will this transaction provide me with value?" is increasingly being replaced with the Age of the Customer hallmark questions about a Seller: "What do I know about their values?" and "Do their values align with mine?"

For example, in the new Age, a Seller's values are appraised by Customers, including, but not limited to, things like:

- *Commitment to the Customer:* In delivering service and/or solving a problem, does the Seller seem more interested in the transaction or the relationship?
- *Customer experience:* How does the Seller respond to negative customer experiences, whether in person or online as UGC?
- *Commitment to the online Community:* Does the Seller behave as a member of related Communities in a way that serves first and sells second? (See "Online Values" on the next page).
- *Commitment to the physical Community:* Whether locally, nationally, or globally, does the Seller demonstrate an interest in something greater than itself?
- *Commitment to the environment:* Does the Seller have a stated position and confirmed demonstration of environmental stewardship and sustainability?

In the Age of the Customer, *value* is what you offer; *values* are how you behave.

Values Appraisal and the Moment of Relevance

Having your values appraised is one thing, but how they're being appraised in the Age of the Customer is another level of scrutiny because of the prime disruptive force of the new Age. Remember the Moment of

Relevance? Let's review how it works:

- Your business is being rejected or accepted online by Users and Prospects even before you know or have access to the appraisers.
- You're being rejected or accepted online by existing Customers before you even know they're interested in buying again.

Leading up to the Moment of Relevance, when an online shopper is winnowing a list of prospective Sellers down to one or two, your classic value proposition—price, product, selection, customization, service, delivery, etc.—is likely only criteria for whether your business makes it to the finals. Once the two finalists are chosen, with so many Seller options in traditional and online marketplaces, it's quite likely that there will be very little—if any—difference in the classic value proposition between them. So how is a decision to be made?

The determining factor at the Moment of Relevance is increasingly based on an appraisal of the Seller's values. And this appraisal is likely to be highly nuanced, maybe even subliminal.

Let's take a look at how a Seller's values might manifest online.

> **THIS WILL BE ON THE TEST**
>
> *Value is the threshold of your relationship with Customers; values are the foundation.*

Online Values

In the Age of the Seller, a business could get away with the ABC approach: Always Be Closing. Crass commercialism was the norm in almost all settings. In the new Age, Users, Prospects, and Customers are more discerning, and from this discernment comes the appraisal of online values.

What is the tone of your online marketing message? Tone is how brand messages are incorporated as you serve any online Community, from crassly commercial ads to almost subliminal messaging when contributing content to an online Community.

Any advertising or product-related messaging is, of course, expected to have a call-to-action angle designed to close the sale. Nothing about the Age of the Customer prevents Sellers from making their best sales effort. But in an online Community environment, the ABC approach is dialed back to anywhere from "Oh, by the way, you might want to consider this," in your own Communities to not a hint of ABC in Communities you join.

In the new Age, since there are many new ways of qualifying Prospects into Customers in the online environment, including prequalifying themselves, there are also new rules. The new rules for appraising your online values occur in the following two Community-related environments.

Communities You Own

The online platforms you own, like your website, blog, YouTube page, Facebook Fan Page, etc., are the places you've created, own, and manage in order to build online Communities. Their purpose is to attract and engage Users and Prospects and, ultimately, create Customers.

Guidelines for establishing and demonstrating compelling online values that correspond to your offline values include:

- Are you using technologies that make online Community-building possible?
- Are you creating an environment where an online Community can flourish around the value you deliver and the values you demonstrate?
- Are your sites easy to navigate? Example: After several clicks on your site, can a visitor easily navigate back to where they started?
- How intrusive are your call-to-action elements, such as pop-up offers? There is a fine line between making helpful suggestions and being abusive.
- Do you make it easy for Users and Customers to ask questions electronically, and do you follow up?
- Do you allow Users and Customers to comment on their experience with your technology, products, service, or any content you post?
- Are you serving, maintaining, and protecting your customer Communities, while accepting that you cannot control the discussion?

> THIS WILL BE ON THE TEST
>
> *Marketing is what you say; values are what you do—especially when no one is watching.*

How much control a Seller is willing to subordinate to Community members is a measure of their values. Inappropriate comments should not be allowed, but critical ones must be.

Communities You Join as a Member

As a Seller, when you become a member of a Community you do not own, other members look at this participation in a different way from Communities you own. The primary values focus in this case is whether you're willing to take part in and contribute to this Community you've joined with more passive and patient marketing goals. Will you allow the only marketing benefits to accrue from the fact that the Community is aware that a member of your company contributed content and expertise to the Community?

In the Age of the Customer, where essentially everything you sell is a commodity, value has become the threshold of a customer Community, as values are becoming the foundation and the new differentiator. In the new Age, Customers are more likely to tell their Communities how they feel about your values than anything else. But remember, that feeling can go either way—positive or negative.

Values, Ethics, Integrity, and Authenticity

Here's another way to think about corporate values: Marketing is what you say, values are what you do—especially when no one is watching.

These three quotes should help you think about values, ethics, integrity, and authenticity/transparency. One is from an ancient philosopher, one from a 20th century Nobel Laureate, and one from a 21st century ethics expert.

Here are all three principles used in one business example: "John, I just discovered that the last point you wanted put in the contract we signed was accidentally left out. But since I told you I would accept it, let's put it back in and re-sign the contract."

If value is the threshold of a Seller's relationship with Customers, values are the foundation of those relationships.

Authenticity/Transparency

The way to live with honor is to be in reality what you appear to be.

—Socrates (5th century B.C.)

Integrity

Integrity has no need of rules.

—Albert Camus

The Myth of Sisyphus (1942)

Ethics

Ethics is devotion to the unenforceable.

—Len Marrella

In Search of Ethics (2005)

Prepare for the Moment of Relevance

While each Customer puts their own emphasis on the major elements of value, the good news is that the concept is not difficult to define. But values, like beauty, are much more in the eye of the beholder.

Once, if you operated your business in such a way as to be able to deliver on the structures of value, you could get your share of the business. But in the Age of the Customer, the intangibles that are part of the structure of values are achieving more interest, scrutiny, and, well, value.

There have been times in my career when I had to compete with liars, cheaters, and unethical people. It seemed incredible to me that anyone could get away with that behavior, not to mention how they could live with themselves. But to paraphrase a passage from the book of Numbers, in the Age of the Customer your sins will find you out.

If you're ethical, honest, or demonstrate other attractive values, congratulations! You'll do well in the new Age.

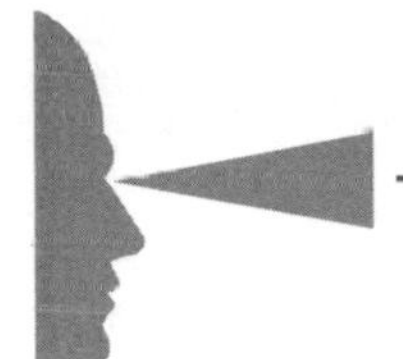

Chapter 8

The Power of Trust

Few things help an individual more than to place responsibility upon him and to let him know that you trust him.

—Booker T. Washington

Thousands of years ago, when Og instinctively held up his open palm for the first time to reveal to Gog that he wasn't holding a weapon, Og was saying "Trust me, I mean you no harm." When Gog believed the message of that gesture and accepted it by holding up his own open palm, the first contract was forged. When humans began choosing trust over fear, they started trading with each other instead of taking what they wanted by force.

So there you have it. The founding element of the marketplace, which has underpinned and underwritten human society, is trust.

Trust was at the headwaters of the Age of the Seller and it will only grow in value in the Age of the Customer. Here are two reasons why:

- It's the right thing to do. Being trustworthy aligns with every faith-based and ethical notion going back thousands of years.
- It's a good business practice. When trust is present, time is saved, productivity goes up, and people are happier.

The opposite of trust, as demonstrated by our two primordial forebears above, is fear. Arky Ciancutti, M.D. is the co-author of *Built on Trust,* and was the original trust guru on my radio program. Arky says fear always runs into the law of diminishing returns, whereas trust multiplies and magnifies itself. This excerpt is from his book:

We are a society in search of trust. The less we find, the more precious it becomes. Along with technology and innovation, trust is one of the most powerful forces in business today. Trust is waiting to be harvested. It's not even low-hanging fruit. It's lying on the ground, there for the taking.

Trust is simply doing what you promised when you promised, and if you cannot do either of those things, you get back with the other person with an update. Arky calls that process "closure."

But trust is also doing what you think others expect of you, even when you don't have to, as I discussed in the ethical examples in chapter 7, "Value and Values." The first time you demonstrate trust with a Customer when they don't expect it will be serendipitous validation of their buying decision. The second time it happens, your Customer will claim a valuable business and emotional return on their investment of trusting you.

Another of my trust experts is Stephen M.R. Covey, the eldest son of the late Stephen Covey. In his book *The Speed of Trust*, Stephen M.R. says,

There is one thing that is common to every individual, relationship, team, family, organization, nation, economy, and civilization throughout the world—trust. It changes the quality of every present moment and alters the trajectory and outcome of every future moment of our personal and professional lives.

You've known about trust all your life and likely have tried to be trustworthy. My goal is to help you recognize trust as the multi-faceted, powerful source of influence that it is, so you make sure it's a conscious component of everything you and your organization does.

THIS WILL BE ON THE TEST

Trust is doing what you think others expect of you, even when you don't have to.

The Velocity of Trust

When I talked about change in the Introduction, I said there's nothing new about it except that its velocity has increased. And this truth is why, as powerful and as important as trust has been in human history, I believe it's going to fulfill Arky's prophecy and be even more precious in the Age of the Customer.

Humans have created technological innovations that would have seemed like magic little more than a generation ago. These are very exciting times, aren't they? But all of this new stuff is useless without a proficient interface between technology and the benefit it promises. And that interface is us—you and me.

But as the form-factor of technology has gotten smaller, faster, and smarter, humans have not. Yes, we've learned more, but human intellect has not advanced at the same velocity as change. As technology's interface partner, humans are still pretty much the same as we were when our greatest levers were fire and a wheel. Consequently, we've had to learn how to not only benefit from technology, but to cope with how it has increased the velocity of change.

Enter Trust

> **THIS WILL BE ON THE TEST**
>
> *In the new Age, B2B Customers are looking for partners more and vendors less.*

As mentioned earlier, trust saves time. If Customers believe they can trust you, they don't have to look for other options, which requires the necessary due diligence. In the case of retail consumers, they don't have to scan through the UGC of a Seller they don't yet know. Because they can trust you, they place their order and move on to the next attempt to manage the velocity of change in their lives. And that's how trust helped you meet their quest for relevance.

In the business-to-business universe, a trust relationship with you almost synthesizes time for your B2B Customers, as demonstrated by this three-step exercise:

1. Try to count the number of times in a month you transact business with a Customer without receiving ongoing instruction or reminders.
2. Think about what you deliver to your B2B Customers, then imagine how many times it comes into play as that Customer's team and their Customers directly or indirectly touch your contribution.
3. Imagine the order that your trustworthiness contributed to. Then consider the chaos that would be created for your Customer if you suddenly failed their trust.

In the new Age, B2B Customers are looking for partners more and vendors less. If you want to be able to claim the trust of Customers, ask yourself if they see you merely as a vendor or an integrated partner connected by the precious concept of trust.

Yes, there are contracts that bind the parties to respective duties and specific performance. But words and signatures on pieces of paper are nothing more if a signer of a contract breaches trust by pushing the envelope of those covenants. Trust is more than delivery and performance. Trust is peace of mind. And a contract may cause someone to perform out of fear of a lawsuit, but it doesn't create trust. Only two humans believing in each other can do that.

Here's how to do your part:

- Handle issues at the lowest possible level. A boss once told me, "When you have an unhappy Customer, do everything you can to solve the problem. Because if they get to me, I'm going to give them whatever they want." Empowering employees to solve problems quickly with the relationship in mind, rather than the transaction, will convey trust to Customers.
- Tell the truth, even if it's bad news. Truth is not only moral, it's simple, efficient, and productive.
- No surprises. Surprises are for birthdays. In the marketplace, most surprises are not good. Arky calls no surprises "closure."
- Manage as a trust role model. Organizational trust is one of those unique intangibles that's influenced by gravity. One thing I learned as an officer in the U.S. Army is, if you want to see how trust is practiced by the commander, talk with one of the privates. The same is true of any organization.

THIS WILL BE ON THE TEST

Tell the truth, even if it's bad news. Truth is not only moral, it's simple, efficient, and productive.

And all of the trust elements and principles you practice on Main Street apply on Cyber Street. You just have to find ways to convey them virtually.

Prepare for the Moment of Relevance

As you know, the message of this book is heavily weighted on the value Customers are increasingly placing on relevance. When a Customer considers doing business with a Seller in the new Age, after they verify the commodity of competitiveness, the last step is establishing relevance.

When people have a difficult time describing something, they may say, "Well, I know what it looks like when I see it." If you ask a Customer what they think is relevant to them, they likely won't know how to answer, because relevance is just something you know when you see it. But it's also something you know when you feel it.

Trust is like that too.

Stephen M.R. Covey proposed that trust is "common to every human interaction." Trust has become so foundational in our lives that we've developed an ability and instinct to assess it literally in a moment, without question or conversation. And in the Age of the Customer, where purchasing decisions are being made at the Moment of Relevance, anything a Seller can do to elicit, demonstrate, and prove trust is as close to perfect as you can get.

THIS WILL BE ON THE TEST

Having an organization that is built on trust is an essential Age of the Customer best practice.

And nowhere does trust flourish better or more abundantly than when delivered by small businesses. There are two reasons:

1. Small business owners know that trust is the best business practice, both from their vendors and to their Customers.
2. On Main Street, where most small businesses live and operate, there is nowhere to hide. And this is especially true in the new Age, with so many others co-owning a Seller's brand message.

All small businesses have to do is stop feeling and acting like marketplace ugly ducklings because of our size, and realize that where trust is a major relevance marker, small businesses actually look like beautiful swans.

Now more than ever, having an organization that is, as Arky says, "built on trust" is not only the right thing to do, it's an essential Age of the Customer best practice that will deliver a return beyond what any other practice or asset could.

When you practice trust, you've laid the foundation for an organization that can be built on trust and that can deliver relevance.

SECTION II

TAKING THE AGE OF THE CUSTOMER TO MARKET

And once you get instantaneous communication with everybody, you have economic activity that's far more advanced, far more liquid, far more distributed than ever before.

—Marc Andreessen
Co-author, Mosaic
First widely-used Internet browser

Section II

Taking The Age of the Customer to Market

In Section I, you were introduced to a once-in-an-eon event: the shift from one marketplace Age to a new one.

We identified numerous ways that the Age of the Customer would change the way the marketplace worked, primarily with regard to the relationship your business has with its Customers. We talked about history, ideas, concepts, dynamics, and paradigm shifts.

Since the Age of the Seller was all we knew for 10,000 years prior to 1993, I feel it necessary to emphasize why it's imperative that you make the transition from being Hidebound, on the way to extinction, to being Visionary, on the way to success you can sustain in the Age of the Customer. Thanks for staying with me.

In Section II, we will focus on specific tips and best practices that you can put to work today as you listen to and respond to the new expectations of Customers. You'll recognize many of the terms, concepts, and shifts already mentioned, but this time they'll be associated with applications as you take your business to market, prepare for the Moment of Relevance, and execute your Age of the Customer strategy.

Even if you are on the right track, you'll get run over if you just sit there.

—Will Rogers

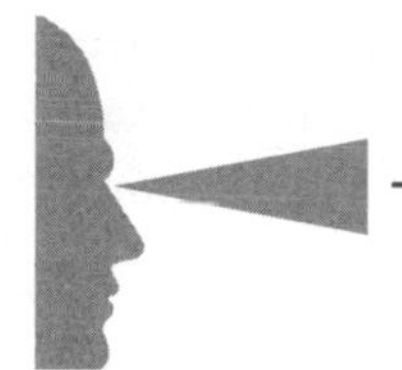

Chapter 9

What's Love Got to Do with It?

It is not the strongest of the species that survive, nor the most intelligent, but the one most responsive to change

—Charles Darwin

People start businesses because of love.

We love to make and sell things: shoelaces, tires, socks, cars, soap, helicopters, computers, bread, air conditioners, etc. You love your business, I love my business. Starting and running a business is a love story.

Yes, I know. Our businesses are not always lovable. Indeed, a business is like a teenager: You may not always like it, but you always love it. Which is a good thing, because if you didn't love your business, you wouldn't come back the day after it gave you the worst day of your life.

As Tina Turner asked in her song, what's love got to do with it? Love is an important component of being in business. But love can also be a problem: Is it possible to love your business too much? As business owners, we know how to fall in love with our businesses, but we don't know how and when to fall out of love with it. Here are two love stories that went wrong:

One of the great stories about American business is the one about how companies in the railroad industry missed many freight-hauling opportunities because they thought they were in the railroad business instead of the transportation business. When freight trucks and better highways came along, the railroads were MIA. In the 20th century, railroad companies loved their business so much that many of them failed.

More recently, you've watched the newspaper industry fall on hard times. Again, the reason is love. Newspaper publishers thought they were in the newspaper business instead of the business of delivering news and commentary by whatever form of access their readers preferred. When the Internet and associated digital applications came along, many newspaper publishers loved their businesses right up to their last issue, and many others have become a mere shadow of their former selves, both in physical size and distribution.

There are many other stories like these two in the history of business. I'm sure you know some yourself. My goal is to make sure this doesn't happen to you, so allow me to reveal something that may one day save your business from a spin-crash-and-burn failure:

BLASINGAME'S LAW OF BUSINESS LOVE

It's okay to fall in love with what you do, but it's not okay to fall in love with how you do it.

Take a look at these small business examples:

- It's okay to love owning a restaurant. But in the Age of the Customer, you're going to need to post your daily menu online, including your mobile site or app. Even if you have the best food (competitiveness), you have to connect with Customers the way they want (relevance).
- It's okay to love owning a tire store. But in the Age of the Customer, where Walmart can sell tires cheaper than you can buy them (competitiveness), you're going to need to create a customer community and contact system (relevance) that allows you to remind Customers when the tires their families ride on need to be checked, rotated, and balanced (values).
- It's okay to love being a wholesale supplier. But in the new Age, your Customers are going to be less interested in a supplier that just drops off products at the loading dock (service). You're going to have to find out how to get your people into the building to deliver your stuff closer to the end user (relevance).

Here are two stories about companies that understood this law.

In 2001 Boeing moved its headquarters to Chicago from Seattle, where it was founded in 1916. Such a bold decision was unimaginable to most in the Seattle community. But Seattle was the seat of Boeing's commercial airline world, and the company wanted to also be seen as a player in the defense and space industries. The leadership believed that if they were going to reinvent their brand, they needed to do it from a new perch, in Chicago. The move may not have been good for Seattle, but it was good for the company. Boeing understood that they should be in love with the aerospace business, including airline manufacturing, but not with Seattle.

In chapter 3, "Parallel Universes," you read the IBM story about how the leadership saved the company by realizing they were not in the computer business, but rather the information business, before it was too late. So the company began to shift from making hardware and software to adding services, which literally saved the company. IBM understood that they should be in love with making and selling digital information management, not just computer stuff.

Prepare for the Moment of Relevance

What do you love about your business? I'm serious; make a list. Write down what you love about your business: the products, the process, the relationships, the challenge, the accomplishment, the community esteem, the financial success, the physical location. Document everything you can, large and small.

When you finish, go back over the list and ask yourself if any of these things might be holding you back right now. You may need some help with this, so engage your team or those who will help you be more objective than you can be on your own. Then go back over the list a second time and try to imagine how any of them could become a problem in the future. Play the "what if" game. As you go through this process, listen for and beware of responses that are the opposite of Blasingame's Law of Business Love:

- "Well, this is how we've always done it."
- "It's been good enough for this company for the last 25 years and I don't see why that's going to change."
- "We built this business from scratch without a website, mobile app, or social media strategy."
- (Your excuse here).

These quotes also make great epitaphs on the tombstone of a dead business.

Love your business, but don't love how you do business.

In the Age of the Seller, competitiveness could take a holiday. In the Age of the Customer, your brand doesn't have that luxury. You're under the relevance microscope 24/7/365, on Main Street and Cyber Street.

—Jim Blasingame

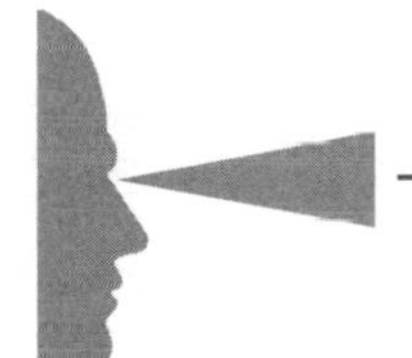

Chapter 10

Defining Brand Relevance

A brand for a company is like a reputation for a person. You earn a reputation by trying to do hard things well.

—Jeff Bezos
Founder, Amazon.com

Perhaps the part of the Age of the Seller that is most closely associated with relevance is the influence of branding.

A Seller works hard and invests as much as possible to stay top of mind with Customers. If the work and investment are successful, an emotional attraction to the Seller's brand is formed. Here's how it works: When a Customer thinks of something she needs, if she has seen or heard a branding message, if she has heard someone else recommend a company or product, and especially if she has already had a good experience with a product or business, that's what pops into her head and causes her to choose that product or company. As my Brain Trust member and branding expert Phil Nulman says, "That's the 'Ding!' in branding."

Here's the good news: In the Age of the Customer, you'll still need to perform—and Customers will still respond and be attracted to—branding activity. But in the new Age, branding has a new component that was introduced earlier in this book—the Moment of Relevance.

Like the brand "Ding!", the Moment of Relevance also happens in the mind of a Customer, but instead of thinking about the logo, tag line, a previous experience with the Seller, etc., this moment is increasingly more practical and less emotional. Take a look at these online examples:

- How easy is the Seller's website to navigate?
- Do they have a mobile site and/or mobile app?
- Is the phone number "hot" so I can easily call on my smartphone?

- Are customer reviews and comments available?
- Are there social media elements?
- Is there e-commerce capability—can I buy now?
- Do they take PayPal?
- How well do they help me help myself?
- (Your relevance requirement here.)

In the Age of the Seller, branding was often the first way a Prospect learned about a business—and this can still happen in the new Age. But as more people use technology to find, become informed about, and buy things, before they get emotionally invested in your brand elements, they may have already ruled you in or out. And their verdict could be over any one of the things above, or any number of other similar points.

> **THIS WILL BE ON THE TEST**
>
> *In the Age of the Seller, your brand could take a holiday. In the Age of the Customer, it doesn't have that luxury.*

Just as Customers experience the "Ding!" differently, every Customer has different Moment of Relevance criteria. Being competitive by delivering value is important, but as I've said before, this is merely table stakes; in the new Age it's not enough. You can be competitive and still lose the business by failing the Moment of Relevance.

Prepare for the Moment of Relevance

If the Age of the Customer is a sword of change, the Moment of Relevance is the tip of that cold steel, indifferent to the very existence, let alone success, of any Seller. In a universe where you're one of potentially thousands of brands trying to get noticed, every Prospect is asking these two rude questions:

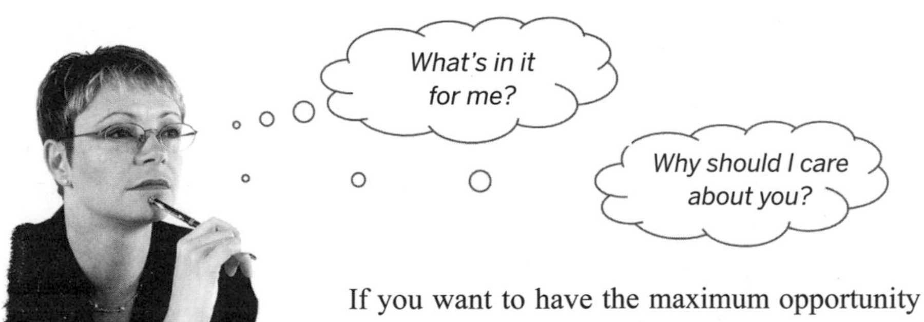

If you want to have the maximum opportunity for your brand to be successful in the Age of the Customer, I recommend doing the following:

- Whatever you do to go to market in the pursuit of your business model, know that every person you hope to influence to buy from you is asking these two questions, consciously or subconsciously, right now.
- On a prominent wall of your office, post an image that represents a Customer, as you see on the previous page, with those two questions as captions in balloons.
- Make sure every employee believes that their professional success depends upon their efforts to address these questions.
- Re-enforce and re-execute the above, plus your own steps every day.

In the Age of the Seller, your brand could take a holiday. In the Age of the Customer, it doesn't have that luxury; you're under the relevance microscope 24/7/365, on Main Street and Cyber Street.

The greatest danger to any brand in the new Age is not being uncompetitive, but rather, being irrelevant.

Brands are publicly shared aspects of culture. Their power derives from the shared public-ness of their various meanings.

—Judie Lannon
Editor, *Market Leader*

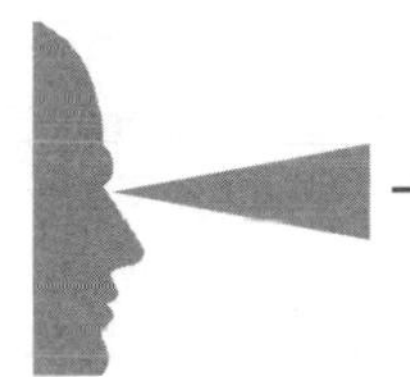

Chapter 11

Brand Ownership

In the Age of the Seller, Customers were acquired and relationships managed through the paradigm of the Seller having control of products, brand messaging, and product information, while Customers owned only the buying-decision element, which included the word-of-mouth factor.

For generations, a brand message could be successful as a work of fiction created by a team of Madison Avenue marketing wordsmiths to motivate and manipulate. And the classic analog word-of-mouth structure was simply no match against most marketing machines.

But in the Age of the Customer, the information element is now increasingly owned by Customers, which, as previously revealed, has shifted the balance of control. And an increasingly powerful component of the information element is what Customers are saying about the products they use and the Sellers they patronize.

In the new Age, there are at least four significant reasons that the best a Seller can do is share control of its brand message with Customers.

1. Meet Your Brand's New Co-owner

Remember those three letters, UGC, first introduced in earlier chapters? User Generated Content sounds benign enough but it represents the two-edged sword by which brands large and small will either flourish or die.

In the new Age, a successful brand message will look less like Madison Avenue manipulation and more like references to first impressions and experiences—both good and bad—being discussed by online customer Communities. The term "reference" is intentional, because the Seller may be able to take advantage of good UGC one day and respond to a negative UGC the next. Since no Seller, product, service, or relationship is perfect, the over-arching goal of a Seller's brand strategy in the Age of the Customer is to have more positive UGC than negative and, if possible, have no unresolved negative UGC.

There is a legal term called "puffery," where a business is allowed some license to exaggerate a claim about itself or a product. For generations, Madison Avenue manipulated us with puffery, and most of the time this manipulation worked. In fact, as Age of the Seller consumers, we allowed ourselves to be manipulated, as marketing messages and commercials actually became part of the sound track of our lives. Here are a few American examples:

"Winston tastes good like a cigarette should."

"Plop, plop, fizz, fizz, oh, what a relief it is."

"See the USA in your Chevrolet."

"Put a tiger in your tank."

"The best part of waking up is Folgers in your cup."

And here are a few that you might find locally.

"Largest inventory in the tri-state area."

"Cleanest hotel rooms in town."

"Freshest salad bar in the area."

Prior to the Internet and UGC, a business could get away with puffery. But today you have to be able to put these claims up against what I call the "Nu-uh!" test.

2. The Power of "Nu-uh!"

The "Nu-uh!" test is the commercial equivalent of fact-checking in the political world. This is what someone posts as UGC when your brand message didn't meet the expectations of this User, Prospect, or Customer. If you say you have the freshest salad bar and one person writes a post that they thought your salad bar was not fresh, that's your new brand message until you fix it.

> THIS WILL BE ON THE TEST
>
> *In the Age of the Customer, your Customers co-own your brand message.*

"Nu-uh!" could be posted to refute your claim in any number of ways, from a well thought-out explanation of their critique of you, to the cut-to-the-chase version, "Dude! Seriously?!" Either way, if you're getting responses like this to your brand messaging, anyone who rebuts you with a "Nu-uh!" is the co-owner of your brand message.

Disregard the power of UGC and the "Nu-uh!" effect at your own peril.

3. Customers Will Limit Messaging Access

Every Baby Boomer remembers when he or she was their father's first remote control, "Get up, boy, and change the channel." Today, virtually every modern human owns and employs ad-avoiding technologies like remote controls, TiVo, and other digital video recorders to play back their favorite TV programs, thus allowing them to skip the commercials.

Sellers will continue to conduct marketing and advertising in the Age of the Customer, but both of these activities will conform to how Customers permit Sellers to interrupt them and, increasingly, that permission will be based on the Seller's appropriate behavior and contribution to a Community.

4. More Community, Less Demographic

The classic Prospect segmentation method for marketing strategies has been to divide the market based on demographics—age, gender, family size, income, occupation, education, religion, race, nationality ... you get the picture. For example:

- White male, 35-54, high school graduate, married with children
- Black female, 21-34, college graduate, single, no children

> **THIS WILL BE ON THE TEST**
>
> *Interests and Community will increasingly trump generational, ethnic, and gender influences.*

No doubt you've noticed the role Community is playing in the Age of the Customer dynamics. In chapter 6, Community was introduced as a new Influencer and a new way to think about prospecting for Customers. And in chapter 7, the power of community values on individual customer purchasing decisions was revealed. The concept here focuses on how a Community can co-own your brand message.

If there's one thing that the Age of the Customer can be defined by, it's that customer behavior will increasingly be influenced by the values of the Communities they associate with and less by demographic nomenclature. In plain language, interests and associated Community involvement will increasingly trump generational, ethnic, and gender influences.

Three new ways to compare a demographic and a Community are:

1. Community involvement by members of a demographic is a profile in humanity—it's what people are excited about at this time in their life.

   Almost every demographic designator is associated with a piece of paper—birth certificate, diploma, marriage license, etc.—words and dates with no humanity.

2. Community evidence is demonstrated with words, action, and money.

   Demographic evidence is kept in a drawer or a safe deposit box.

3. Community is where a person is now and is going.

   A person's demographic represents where they've been.

In the Age of the Seller, using a demographic profile would get you close enough to be reasonably successful. In the new Age, technology fosters customer Communities based on interests and values, not dates on paper. Customer acquisition will demand the following about Communities versus demographics:

> **THIS WILL BE ON THE TEST**
>
> *UGC represents the two-edged sword by which brands, large and small, will live and die.*

- Communities are smaller and change faster than a demographic.
  - Unlike demographics, Communities communicate and interact.
  - Behavior will be increasingly influenced by relationships and experiences.
- Communities create and share information and experiences (UGC).
  - This is word of mouth on steroids.
  - It is also more powerful and potentially viral than any marketing/branding message—a two-edged sword.
- Communities resist the manipulation of Age of the Seller marketing and advertising strategies.
  - UGC trumps Madison Avenue.
  - Marketing messages are scrutinized and verified.
  - Sellers share brand message ownership with Users and Customers.
- Communities prefer Sellers that consistently perform with compatible values.

- Commercial advantage accrues from Community participation and contribution instead of messaging.
- Value is the threshold of a Community.
- Values are the foundation of a Community.

Good News for Small Business—Not So Much for Big Business

The shifts in brand ownership will hit big businesses hard, because they rely on the Madison Avenue transaction approach rather than the relationship approach. Virtually by definition, for a big business to move the sales needle they have to paint the market with a very broad brush, which is difficult in the granularity of a Community.

For small firms, the brand ownership shift is good news, because Customers are increasingly responding less to mass marketing and more to what small businesses have always been good at: values-based, relationship-building, Community associated, granular interactions and word of mouth.

This is not to say that big business can't figure this out and make adjustments. They will and they are. It's just that it will take them longer and it will be more complicated and frustrating for them than it will be for small business.

Prepare for the Moment of Relevance

Regardless of whether the new brand ownership dynamic is good news or not, one thing is without question: The ownership influences are coming from sources that did not exist in the original Age.

Where you once had to deal with the influence of Customers only, in the Age of the Customer, brand ownership pressure could come from many interlopers, including one or both of the new Influencers: Users and Communities. Consequently, how you present your business to the marketplace, both in person and online, has to pass through the much finer filters of accuracy, honesty and relevance. To paraphrase the Miranda rights, anything you say—and post and do—can and will be attributed to you.

> **THIS WILL BE ON THE TEST**
>
> *Customers are responding less to mass marketing and more to values-based Communities.*

Your job is to make sure your brand co-owners support, confirm, and repeat your marketing messages. And once again, this job is not a temporary means to an end, but a permanent way of life.

Chapter 12

Evolution of Expectations

Evolution is not something that simply applies to life; it applies to the whole universe.

—John Polkinghorne
Physicist, theologian, and author

When describing what influences the behavior of individuals as they pursue their lives, you would likely include words and concepts associated with goals, plans, passion, desire, ego, personality, etc. In matters of human interaction, as we meet, love, and work together, there is often an abiding struggle between my passion and your ego, for example, or your goals and my plans. More often than not, long-term personal relationships are based more on my tolerance of you today and your forbearance of me tomorrow.

But in the marketplace, affection and sentiment give way to performance and contracts, because tolerance and forbearance are subjective, inefficient, and unproductive. Consequently, a very powerful concept has developed over the millennia that is the nucleus of how marketplace participants reconcile differences and find common ground. In classically efficient marketplace style, this concept has been reduced to one simple word: expectations.

For example, the most important thing for you to know about someone with whom you're negotiating a contract is that party's expectations—especially that one, true, uncompromising expectation, beyond which they won't go. But nowhere has the quest for expectations been more evident and well developed than between Seller and Customer. Because the quicker a Customer's expectations about value and values can be determined, the quicker the Seller can find a way to fulfill those expectations and make the sale.

The interesting, and sometimes maddening, thing about expectations is that they change. Not just from one person to the next, but by each person. I want chocolate ice cream today, but tomorrow I might want strawberry. You may want a convertible car today but need to trade it in for a minivan next year. These are changes in personal preferences that are not going away.

Making the Expectations Shift

Now let's talk about the evolution of customer expectations and how your business practices have to adjust and conform. As you can see from Figure 7, as the Age of the Seller succumbs to the Age of the Customer, an evolution of expectations is occurring and it has many influences, including technology, community, new information sources, etc. This new information demonstrates how, in addition to having to make adjustments to meet any Customer's individual expectations, you also have to deal with how Age of the Customer expectations are evolving and changing the way you find, contact, qualify, and acquire Customers.

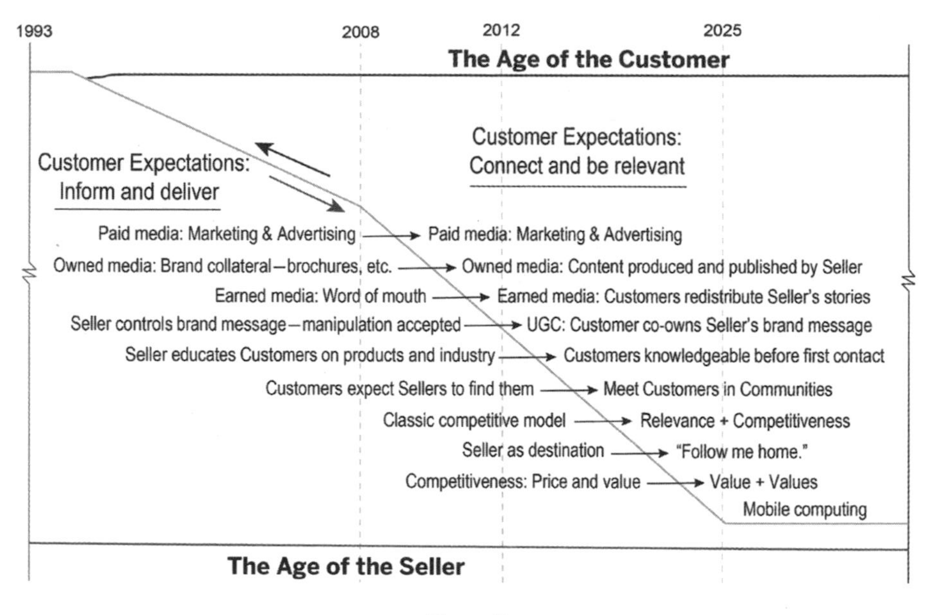

Figure 7

The good news is that essentially all activity you would have performed to meet customer expectations in the Age of the Seller has a corresponding—but newly evolved—activity in the Age of the Customer. But, as is the theme throughout this book, new customer expectations now require that business practices are concentrated more on the Customer's terms than ever before. And it isn't enough just to learn how to adapt to these new expectations;

you will be required to constantly check in with Customers to see how their expectations have changed since the last time you made contact with them, even if it was just last week.

What follows is a more detailed narrative of the side-by-side listing in Figure 7. This list is intentionally more macro than granular in order to help you begin to understand how to adjust your planning and execution.

Evolution of Customer Expectations

Age of the Seller	Age of the Customer
In the original Age, Customers expected a Seller to primarily inform them about their offerings, make the delivery, and provide service.	In the new Age, Customers already have most of the information they need but want Sellers to connect with them in a way that is relevant.
Paid Media	
Classic marketing and advertising perfected in the 20th century.	Sellers will still conduct marketing and advertising strategies, but they will be merely one of the disciplines in a much larger array of Customer acquisition disciplines.
Owned Media	
Brand collateral, such as brochures.	Every Seller—large or small—has to become a publisher of content it creates, produces, and distributes over a number of internal and external channels, especially digital channels.
Earned Media	
Classic referrals and simple word of mouth.	Customers are publishers too, so when they redistribute a Seller's content to their communities, that becomes referrals and word of mouth on steroids.
Control of Message	
Brand messaging was wholly owned by Sellers, varied from legal puffery to outright manipulation, and was generally accepted by Customers.	Due to the proliferation of UGC, Users, Prospects, Customers, and Communities co-own a Seller's brand message. Customers increasingly place highest credibility on the comments of other Influencers.

→

Age of the Seller	Age of the Customer
Product Information	
Almost all information a Customer used to make a buying decision was acquired from the Seller.	Customers often have acquired virtually all the information they need to make a buying decision before they make first contact with a Seller.
First Contact	
Customers were more likely to become acquainted with a Seller through some type of activity in the marketplace: shopping, marketing, advertising, or demographic research.	Sellers are increasingly as likely to make first contact with Customers based on involvement in an online Community as through traditional marketing activity.
Information Exchange	
Most information exchange occurs with significant involvement by Seller.	Having control of most of the information needed to make a buying decision, Customers are calling the shots on how they acquire and where they consume a Seller's information.
Competitiveness	
The classic value proposition of product, price, selection, service, etc., is the prime determinant of competitiveness.	Now much more multi-faceted, competitiveness includes the value proposition as a threshold expectation, but is increasingly trumped by relevance and an appraisal of values.

Up to now, every original Age business practice listed has a corresponding practice in the new Age. In other words, the only things different are the new versions of former practices as a result of the influences of the new Age.

But did you notice something was missing from the Evolution of Expectations table above? In fact, it is such a new capability that it qualifies as an outlier, a killer app, and a paradigm shifter. The thing that can pull off this Age of the Customer hat trick is mobile computing, a.k.a. mobile.

There is no Age of the Seller activity that corresponds to mobile and, consequently, it deserves its own chapter (chapter 13, "Global Mobile").

Prepare for the Moment of Relevance

In the Age of the Seller, the marketplace was driven by consumption created by innovation. And all of this was around products and services produced and delivered by Sellers to Customers who essentially became passive recipients of the next innovation. Think of all the new things Customers have been able to acquire for the first time in the past century: cars, kitchen appliances, radios, televisions, personal computers, and iPods, just to name a few.

In the Age of the Customer, most of the innovations Customers acquire are less likely to be new things as new empowerment. Rather than Customers getting excited over a new tangible thing, they're more likely to get excited about a new app for their smartphone that helps them find, review, compare, shop for, buy, and take delivery of an even newer thing.

> **THIS WILL BE ON THE TEST**
>
> *Only one thing can pull off the Age of the Customer hat trick—mobile.*

So new acquisitions are more about Customers increasing influence and control over their participation in the marketplace, and less about what's being acquired in that participation. Consequently, customer expectations become less about what you sell and more about how you can make a transaction handy, convenient, time-saving, on-demand, pre-appraised, on multiple platforms, in multimedia, etc. As I've said, this is a big part of the definition of relevance, and it's the new expectation of Customers.

As the risk of repeating myself, but not apologizing for doing so, relevance is the coin of the realm in the Age of the Customer. Being competitive is merely table stakes. Disregard those two truths at your own peril.

God meant us to be wireless. The last cord we were connected to was cut at birth.

—Dr. Frank Sanda
founder, Japan Communications

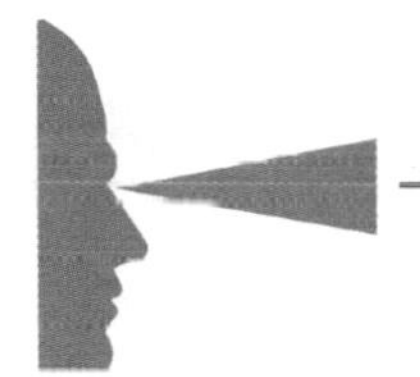

Chapter 13

Global Mobile

The future of computing is mobile.

Eric Schmidt, former CEO of Google
Atmosphere, April 2010

In 1998, I began interviewing technology experts on my radio program about an emerging alternative to dial-up Internet connection: broadband, a.k.a. "big pipes."

In those days, virtually all residential and business connections to the Internet were made over a phone line, or POTS (plain old telephone service), with the help of an external modem whose speed was measured in terms of kilobits per second—usually less than 56 kbs. Broadband Internet connection, measured in megabits per second, was in less than 4% of households and almost no businesses.

At that time, I made the prediction that when broadband Internet became ubiquitous and broadly adopted, the world would change. Appraising the explosion of interest in and adoption of all things online in the waning days of the 20th century, even at the snail's pace of a dial-up connection over a 1200 baud modem, I believed we were on the threshold of an exciting era of new opportunities, whose companion would be a comparable level of disruption.

Soon after that, I started reporting on and talking about technological convergence, which is the process of aggregating innovations into shared devices, platforms, and connectivity. I said: "If you want to see technological convergence take place before your eyes, watch the cell phone industry." This was just prior to Research In Motion's addition of voice capability to their Blackberry email device.

Even though I envisioned how the power of broadband Internet would significantly alter our world, and even though I could see that cell phones were going to be handier because they would get more robust, I must confess that in those days I did not fully grasp the shifts that would take place when broadband converged with cell phones.

Yes, I used the word "ubiquitous" in my prophecy, which could have given me cover to claim a mobile broadband prediction. But the truth is, in 1998, my broadband perspective was still tethered to the desktop by an Ethernet cord. In this chapter you're going to learn why your future is cordless.

Back to the Future

Of course, when DSL Internet connections became available from telecom companies and cable companies started bundling Internet connection with their television offerings, the world did change. But now that Internet broadband has made it to Customers living at what the carriers call "the last mile," that shift is old news.

Before we go on, let's address the role of wireless Internet (WiFi) as it contributed to the ubiquity of broadband Internet. Of course, wireless Internet was a very powerful addition to the broadband revolution. When converged with laptop computers, WiFi created many new opportunities to be untethered from the desktop in our personal and professional endeavors.

> **THIS WILL BE ON THE TEST**
>
> *The mother of all disruptions occurred when mobile devices could access the Internet.*

Eventually, WiFi converged with the cell phone. But the mother of all broadband disruptions was born when mobile devices were able to access the Internet over various mobile networks. Even though they were initially not as fast as WiFi, mobile networks cast a larger coverage footprint, which made connecting to the Internet more … well, mobile. And back to my prediction: Broadband ubiquity, today thy name is mobile.

Global Mobile

Here's another thing happening today that has never happened before in the history of the world: People from virtually every walk of life on Planet Earth are acquiring the same thing, at the same time, for the first time. They're buying features-rich, application-ready, Internet-connected mobile devices—a.k.a. smartphones.

Millions of Earthlings are acquiring smartphones that use mobile networks and/or WiFi to connect to the Internet and gain access to other World Wide Web resources. And of course, to connect with other people. While the pace of conversion from regular cell phones to smartphones has been progressive, this process will gain new energy, as it is now no more expensive to make a smartphone than a dumb one. Consequently, any price barrier to adoption of a smartphone has collapsed. All new handheld devices are "smart."

First-world consumers are upgrading to smartphones because of all the cool apps. In America, where consumerism was born, smartphones are changing how we access information, buy things, and connect with our Communities. Business owners and managers around the world are trading in their older, less robust mobile models for smartphones in order to gain access to increasingly handy mobile apps. Business people are now making trips taking no more technology than a device they can put in the pocket of their jeans.

And as millions of citizens of second- and third-world countries acquire a smartphone, it becomes their very first computer and will connect them to the Internet for the first time in their lives. Before owning a house, a microwave, or a car, many will join the 21st century marketplace of ideas and stuff through the power of a device they can hold in the palm of their hand.

> **THIS WILL BE ON THE TEST**
>
> *Unlike the passive "lean back" of TV, or the active "lean forward" of the PC, mobile is "pull it forward"—interactive, up close, personal, and always on.*
>
> —Chuck Martin
> *The Third Screen*

From a Park Avenue penthouse to a village in Venezuela, the shift to mobile connecting and computing is turning steeply upward. For Main Street small businesses from Beijing to Bakersfield, mobile computing is increasing the velocity of what I have said is the preeminent shift of the Age of the Customer: classic marketplace competitiveness is being trumped by relevance. And as consumers become untethered and mobile, they feel increasingly empowered—and they like it.

In chapter 12, I made the point that virtually everything you will do to be successful in the Age of the Customer is a variation on something you did in the Age of the Seller, except for mobile. Mobile computing is truly a unique, 21st century, Age of the Customer force which, on the opportunity/disruption scale, has no peer.

Your business will increasingly find opportunity, or be disrupted by, the convergence of the following two Age of the Customer elements:

- The new business differentiation coin of the realm is relevance.
- The Moment of Relevance is increasingly being defined by customer expectations using mobile computing.

Here are two mobile stories that prove these points. The first one is about access and timing, and the second one is how access to information determines relevance.

The Golf Ball Promotion

A golfer buys golf equipment from two primary sources: his local club pro shop and a golf retailer an hour away. The golfer has given both of these businesses his email address, mobile number, and payment information, including permission to bill him for purchases.

One day, on the way to his club to play golf, the golfer receives a text from the out-of-town retailer about a special offer from a golf ball manufacturer, including a big discount and a customization service. The text read: "Titleist has a "buy 3 get 4 dozen" golf ball offer and they will put your name or initials on the balls. Do you want to order?" In reply, the golfer simply typed one letter, "Y," and made a purchase.

When the golfer got to his club, he asked the pro about the Titleist promotion and was told that he could get the same deal from the pro shop. Unfortunately, a deal had already been made.

Here's the Moment of Relevance opportunity/disruption lesson:

- The golfer didn't care which Seller he bought golf balls from.
- The promotion was identical for both Sellers, so there was no competitive advantage.
- The successful Seller took advantage of information about, and access to, the Customer and helped him make a purchase by simply pressing the "Y" key for "Yes" on his smartphone.

- Timing, access, and convenience are prime relevance expectations in the Age of the Customer.

Everybody Likes Italian

Two Italian restaurants are in the same neighborhood in Peoria, Illinois and both have websites. The first restaurant is more expensive but does not make its own pasta. The second is less expensive and all of its pasta is made fresh onsite, every day.

A couple is visiting from out of town and looking for Italian food. He selects "voice search" on his smartphone and says, "Italian restaurants in Peoria," whereupon both of our restaurants appear as being nearby.

What happens in the next 30 seconds is the Moment of Relevance.

As our Italian food searcher holds this magic wand in his hand and they consider the two websites on the tiny screen, how are they going to choose which restaurant to patronize? Well, one of the restaurants has a mobile site and the other one doesn't. So they choose the one that has a mobile site that presents properly in the aspect ratio of the smartphone, has an easy-to-read menu, and a "hot" phone number he can touch to call for information and make reservations.

The restaurant that got the business was the one that was more expensive and probably didn't have the best pasta, but it was relevant to the prospect. The other one—with the homemade pasta and lower prices—was not chosen simply because it was not ready for mobile primetime, even though it was actually more competitive.

Here's the Moment of Relevance opportunity/disruption lesson:

- This couple made a purchasing decision without either business knowing they even exist.

Your Mobile World

Somewhere a Seller is experiencing an anxiety attack, because he just discovered two things:

- Half of the Prospects and Customers in his market cannot find his business.
- Half of the calls his Prospects and Customers want to make to his business aren't getting through.

Pretty scary, huh? Glad that's not your nightmare, right? Well, if you don't have a mobile strategy, you are that business owner, whether you know it or not. Every day that goes by without your business addressing the increasing demand by Prospects and Customers for information and connectivity over mobile devices and networks is a day closer to that scenario being about your business.

So what are these mobile consumers doing on the tiny screens of these magic wands called smartphones? Besides making calls, texting, and sending emails, they are:

> **THIS WILL BE ON THE TEST**
>
> *Every day you fail to address the mobile expectations of Customers is a day closer to irrelevance.*

- Shopping online—making decisions about what they want and who to buy it from, including online content from Sellers and UGC.
- Navigating to businesses—the one they chose while shopping, or the one previously unknown to them that pops up in their local search.
- Requesting that a picture of a product be texted to them before they drive to the business.
- Buying stuff—using PayPal, credit card, or internal charge in the case of an established account.

But in order to be the "chosen one" by smartphone users, your business has to be mobile ready. That means having all of your business information and resources compatible with the smartphone form factor and technology in at least two ways:

1. Online information is optimized for mobile search, especially local search. Remember "Italian restaurants in Peoria"?
2. A mobile website that automatically presents when your URL is requested from a smartphone.

In the Age of the Customer, where being relevant to Customers trumps being competitive, every business must be fully accessible and high-functioning regardless of how a Prospect or Customer wants to connect with you. And every day that connection is increasingly being requested and relevance is being appraised from a device in the palm of the hand.

Mobile App vs. Mobile Site

As you get your business ready for mobile primetime, one of the decisions you should make is whether to invest in a mobile app or a mobile site. Here's the difference:

Mobile App: This is an application that downloads from the Seller to present information to the Customer.

- *Advantage:* Once the information is downloaded, like an article, photo, or menu, it is not beholden to Internet speed or connection in order to be used.
- *Disadvantage:* A Seller's updated information has to be downloaded.

Mobile Site: This is just a Seller's regular website information modified to fit in the smaller window of a mobile device, whether smartphone or tablet. When a Seller's website is requested from a mobile device, the mobile site will automatically be presented. The mobile site will typically feature the most important elements of the regular website, but with fewer graphics and HTML styling. In other words, form follows function.

> **THIS WILL BE ON THE TEST**
>
> *Not all small businesses need a mobile app, but all need a mobile website.*

- *Advantages:* A customized button can be placed on a mobile device screen that looks just like an app button. All the updated information is available every time the site is requested. It's faster and costs the Seller less to create, update, and maintain than to create a mobile app.
- *Disadvantages:* Mobile sites are not as sexy as most mobile apps. Customers can't use a mobile site unless the device is connected to the Internet.

As a rule, most Sellers, especially small businesses, don't need a mobile app. Having a mobile site will get you ready for mobile prime time just fine. My mobile rule of thumb is: Not all businesses need a mobile app, but every business needs a mobile website.

Prepare for the Moment of Relevance

Let's say you and I are walking toward each other on the street, and I want to tell you about the marketplace paradigm shift taking place between the two Ages. But since I only have the five seconds it takes to pass by within earshot, I can only tell you the single most important thing about the shift. I would tell you the following truth found in:

BLASINGAME'S LAW OF MOBILE COMPUTING

Nothing about your past was mobile. Everything about your future will be mobile.

Going forward you must create a mobile component for every traditional task you do in your business. And any future innovations you develop will be created as mobile resources first and adapted to non-mobile as needed.

Regardless of what you do, what you sell, how you sell it, how you deliver it, or how you service it, the Moment of Relevance is increasingly happening with a device your Customers are holding in their hand.

Any questions?

Chapter 14

"Follow Me Home" A Gift from Customers

Many years ago I was talking to the executive director of a state banking organization about helping his members get more Customers. I've never forgotten one of the things he said to me: "If my member banks would make sure every existing customer they have has all the financial services they need, they wouldn't need a new customer for five years." The basic premise of his thinking is especially true today in the Age of the Customer.

Every business loves new Customers, but do you love them more than existing Customers? Do you work harder and spend more resources acquiring new Customers than you do staying connected to existing Customers? When you advertise, do you assume existing Customers always see your ads or are sitting around waiting for your next ad to appear?

For generations it's been a maxim that it's less expensive to keep an existing Customer than acquire a new one. But keeping the attention of an existing Customer is getting harder and harder, isn't it? Let's talk about one way to turn this challenge into an opportunity.

Who Hijacked My Customer?

In the Age of the Seller there was less competitive pressure and Customers needed you more, so they were more likely to be loyal to the business that provided them with the products and services they needed. Then the Internet came along and brought with it millions of websites.

You had a website built for your business, too. It was beautiful, you were so proud of it, and when you got in the habit of telling people to "Go to our website," it made you feel as if you had your 21st century business bases covered. And this worked for a while.

Then online marketers started bombarding your Customers with a gazillion offers, including alternatives to exactly what you sold your Customers last year or last week or yesterday. As these guys got more sophisticated, Customers increasingly received offers targeted to their interests and purchase history, including from businesses they didn't even know. Consequently, Customers are now increasingly more likely to be interrupted, diverted, or just plain hijacked on their way to calling you, coming to your store, or even going to your website.

In the new Age, Customers still wake up thinking about something they need or want, just like before. But today when Customers decide to shop for and buy something you sell, unless they have a compelling reason to do otherwise, they're going to search online to see what's available. But that activity will be met with a great noise of offerings. And make no mistake; you're part of that noise. Your Customer retention mission is to be such a sweet and familiar sound in that cacophony that eventually they turn to you before anyone else gets a shot at them.

> **THIS WILL BE ON THE TEST**
>
> *Keeping the attention of an existing Customer is getting harder and harder.*

But sweetness requires you to be top-of-mind with exactly what Customers want and make it available to them at that critical point in time: the Moment of Relevance. One of the ways you accomplish this sweet timing is with what I call a "Follow-me-home" strategy. And to help you remember this strategy, here's ...

> **BLASINGAME'S LAW OF CUSTOMER RETENTION**
>
> *It's not your Customer's job to keep your business top-of-mind.*

The Gift of "Follow Me Home"

It's very gratifying when Prospects and Customers come to your business or visit your website, isn't it? But in the Age of the Customer, you cannot depend on that happening, and that's where "Follow me home" comes in. Here's the good news: it's not complicated, you just have to do it.

"Follow me home" is a gift. It means you've asked for and been given permission by a Customer to send them digital communications: email, text, social media, and the next digital communication platform or application that is invented in the future. One of the reasons a "Follow-me-home" strategy is essential in the Age of the Customer is because of ...

BLASINGAME'S NEW LAW OF WEBSITES

Your website is becoming less of a destination for Customers and more of a distribution center.

This "Follow-me-home" gift comes with conditions and responsibilities:

- You must protect the Customer's privacy.
- You can't abuse the gift by over-contacting them or deluging them with commercial offers.
- You must focus on contributing useful content to the recipient first, followed by an offer associated with that content. Think of it this way: Contribute first, sell second.

THIS WILL BE ON THE TEST

The definition of "home" has changed.

In fact, some effective "Follow-me-home" strategies have regular distributions that only contribute content and the only commercial reference is the sender's logo. Remember, the purpose of this strategy is to stay top of mind with sweet relevance that overpowers the noise. When you accomplish this, any commercial messages will be welcomed by Customers receiving your distribution.

But here are the "Follow-me-home" questions you have to answer: Distribute where? Where are my Customers? Where do they take delivery of our distribution? Where is "home"?

Home Isn't Where It Used to Be

Remember when you thought of calling someone and imagined them picking up the phone while sitting in their business or at home? Well, that was another nice trip down Memory Lane, wasn't it?

This is one of the most important things to remember about the difference between the Age of the Seller and the Age of the Customer: The definition of "home," as it relates to where people connect with each other, as well as where they shop and consider their next purchase, has changed. As cell phones proliferated, people started realizing that they were less likely to call *places* and more likely to call *people* wherever they are.

When a Customer gives a Seller permission to "Follow me home," they're talking about their email inbox, their text inbox, or one of the social media platforms. And yes, all of these "homes" today are very likely to be at a location that is unique to the Age of the Customer: in the palm of their hand in the form of a smartphone.

With all of the smartphones in use now, instead of merely calling someone, we actually have connection options as fits the circumstances. And when it comes to Customers, we have to connect based on their relevance expectations. Sellers have to ask Customers how they prefer to be contacted: "Mrs. Smith, we would like to be able to keep you updated on information about how to use our products, plus any special offers we have. How would you like for us to do that?"

THIS WILL BE ON THE TEST

Customers are attracted to Sellers who understand the power of relevance.

Here are two ways Customers are followed home:

1. The first example is the technical definition of "Follow me home": permission-based marketing. The Seller has been given specific permission to send information and offers, including the contact method. This is the high-percentage play.
2. The second example is basically spam. Any offer received that was not requested is spam. There was a time when all spam was bad, but it must be said that today people have become more tolerant of unsolicited email if it comes from Sellers they recognize. So, is there now good spam and bad spam? Are Customers more forgiving of relevant offers, even if they didn't give the Seller permission to send it? Proceed with caution.

Once someone determines they like your business, they're likely to give permission for you to follow them home with digital information and content, by email (newsletters), texting (updates), social media (useful content), etc. But in almost every case, you have to ask them for permission, verbally or digitally.

"Follow me home" supports three critical elements in 21st century customer relationships:

Three Relationship Elements of "Follow Me Home"

Emotional: At the heart of "Follow me home" is trust that a business won't abuse this privilege. This is a gift—value, protect, and perform on this.

Practical: "Follow me home" conveys that you understand Customers are busy and want to stay informed without having to work too hard. So you're being relevant to them by following them home with information and offers they have expressed an interest in.

Technical: Elements on your website that make "Follow me home" easy. For example, "Subscribe to our free newsletter" or "Follow us on Twitter" score the online hat trick: values, thought-leadership, and technical capability.

"Follow me home" is good for your business in four ways:

1. You've been invited to connect with regular, useful content, and appropriate marketing messages.
2. Since it's a natural law that a Prospect has to see several impressions before converting to a Customer, "Follow me home" becomes an effective and efficient conversion practice.
3. "Follow me home" is one of the best ways Users pre-qualify themselves as Prospects.
4. New technologies make delivering on "Follow me home" easier than ever, especially for small businesses.

Part of being relevant is to make it easy for Users, Prospects, and Customers to give you permission to "Follow me home."

Prepare for the Moment of Relevance

In the Age of the Customer, it's not the Customer's job to keep your business top of mind. Consequently, their most likely path will lead to a search, which potentially puts millions of other websites ahead of yours unless you do something to stop this interference.

Customers are increasingly attracted to being served by Sellers that understand the principles and power of relevance in the new Age. Go re-read the golf ball story on page 92. That's a perfect example of how a Seller was relevant to me and got my business by following me home.

Permission to "Follow me home" is given by Users, Prospects, and Customers to Sellers they believe can be trusted to play by the rules, which includes delivering relevant information as instructed. Plus, "Follow me home" will increasingly be seen by Customers as a way to save time in acquiring what they're interested in, whether it's something they use regularly or for the first time in the future.

Every year, people of all walks of life are increasingly valuing their time more than their money. Consider:

BLASINGAME'S LAW OF CUSTOMER TIME

In the Age of the Customer, the most important and relevant thing a Seller can do for Customers is to save them time.

A buying signal is what a Customer gives a salesperson that says he or she is becoming predisposed to do business with that salesperson. One of the greatest sins of any salesperson is to miss a buying signal.

"Follow me home" is a buying signal waiting to happen. Are you listening?

Chapter 15

Emotional Relevance

When dealing with people, remember you are not dealing with creatures of logic, but creatures of emotion.

—Dale Carnegie
Author and self-improvement icon

The two primary sectors of Customers in the marketplace are consumers and businesses. (There is a third, government, but that's another book.) Consequently, as you likely know, it's handy to use the following acronyms when discussing the focus of a Seller's business model: B2C (business to consumer) and B2B (business to business).

Restaurants and clothing stores are B2C examples, while manufacturers and freight haulers are B2B focused. Some Sellers cross over, such as an electrical supply house that serves local industries but also has a "City desk" where individuals can walk up and make a purchase, or a construction company that will build your house but also bids on commercial projects.

Regardless of their focus, they all have this imperative in common: Find, qualify, sell to, and keep Customers that will allow them to make a profit.

This chapter delivers the essence of what Customers in each of these sectors are looking for, but are not likely to tell you directly. And the beauty of that truth is that by serving Customers at that level, without having to be told, you can forge something powerfully relevant: an emotional connection—even with B2B Customers. Think of it like this: Out of the blue, someone in your life tells you they love you and "a moment" happens. In the marketplace, when you deliver what I'm going to reveal to you next, it's where a Moment of Relevance happens. Congratulations! You created it and you get the points.

B2C Relevance

Spend time in the marketplace and you'll have many close encounters of the third kind with the most interesting species in all of nature: the human being. And just as we have learned about the nature of other animals, we also know that the nature of humans isn't much different: All need to breathe, eat, drink, procreate, and survive.

But there is something that clearly sets humans apart from all other fauna: sentience. And one of the manifestations of being self-aware is that beyond whatever humans need, they also want. The most essential fact any Seller must understand about the nature of those very important humans—Customers—is the difference between what they need and what they want.

THIS WILL BE ON THE TEST

What Customers want is somewhere between "a little bit more" and "everything."

Every human who owns an automobile will need to buy new tires at some point, but what they want is to not blow an entire Saturday finding and acquiring tires. So if you own a small business that sells tires, should you advertise your tires, which are commodities and, therefore, very much like those of your competitors? Or should you develop a marketing program and customer information strategy that anticipates when a Customer's tires need replacing and handle that project for them, including pick-up and delivery?

How about this tagline? "New tires *and* your Saturday back." Everyone won't pay more for this service, but the people who want their Saturdays back will.

Basically the hairless weenies of the animal kingdom, human beings need shelter. Modern humans need a house, but what we want is a home. So if you're a realtor, should you focus your message on the obligatory list of a house's features, or how the physical setting and interior space fit what you've learned is your Customer's sense of what a home should be? Try this on:

"Mrs. Johnson, countertops can be replaced. What I want to know is how much will you enjoy the sun rising over that ridge as you enjoy your first cup of coffee every morning?"

Humans, like thousands of other warm-blooded species, need to eat every day, whether they get to or not. But unlike other animals, only humans want to dine. So if you own a fine dining restaurant, do you emphasize the food that will soon be forgotten, or the atmosphere that can create a memory? Check this out:

"Long after you've forgotten how wonderful our food is, you'll still remember the romantic booth near the fireplace."

In the Age of the Customer, the difference between delivering what Customers want and trying to sell them stuff you think they need is, to invoke Mark Twain's wisdom again, "like the difference between lightning and a lightning bug."

Here are two truths:

1. What Customers want is somewhere between "a little bit more" and "everything."
2. Customers will pay more for what they want than they will for what they need.

And when you deliver what Customers want, you get two very valuable things:

1. Customer loyalty
2. Higher profit margins

Consider:

BLASINGAME'S LAW OF B2C RELEVANCE

If you want to have profitable retail Customers for life, give them what they want, not what they need.

And the good news is that small businesses can deliver on what Customers want better than anyone else. The bad news is that too often small business owners forget that the price war is over and they lost, and, consequently, don't charge enough to achieve those higher margins. Your special sauce is your "give Customers what they want" strategy. But it's only special for you if you charge enough for it to achieve a sustainable profit margin.

Remember, you will find Customer relevance closer to what they want than to what they need. Find out what Customers want and then deliver that! And let the Big Box competitors fight the price wars over what they need.

B2B Relevance

When you take a photograph, the resulting product is two-dimensional: tall, wide, and flat. But in most cases, you want the photo to actually show depth, where images in the foreground and background are all in focus.

In photographic terms, the range of focus front to back is called depth of field. And the way to expand depth of field so more of the subjects in the photo are in focus is to add light. Light creates depth of field.

If you were given a photo of people who were the most critical to your success, you'd easily recognize your Customers in the foreground in perfect focus. But as you look deeper into the photo you would notice the images behind that first row increasingly drop out of focus with each receding row. These are your Customer's Customers. The reason for the blur is because for most of the history of the marketplace, Sellers have gotten away with having a very narrow Customer depth of field—just the first row.

When the B2B coin of the realm was to just be competitive, Sellers spent all their time thinking about and serving the faces in the foreground of their photo: their Customers. But as revealed previously, being competitive has been trumped by being relevant. And in the Age of the Customer, perhaps the most important component of being relevant to business Customers is helping them serve the most important person in their photo: their Customers.

Let me say that again with …

BLASINGAME'S LAW OF B2B RELEVANCE

If you want to have profitable business Customers for life, help your Customers help their Customers.

The way to accomplish this is to increase the depth of field of your photo and bring more Customers into focus. Here's a three-step process that works every time:

1. Identify the Customer of your Customer.
2. Find out what your Customer needs to do to become relevant to their Customer.
3. Whatever the answer to #2 is, help your Customer do that.

Executing this approach is how you acquire Customers you almost can't run off. Because when you help your Customers help their Customers, they know you're doing more than just delivering stuff; you've become part of their team, integrated and committed, like a true stakeholder. And this belief creates an emotion that is as close as a business Customer gets to the feeling a consumer has when they get what they want without having to ask for it.

And if you want to pull off the customer relevance hat trick, light up the third row of your business's photo and help your Customers help their Customers help their Customers.

I've done it. It's a beautiful thing.

Prepare for the Moment of Relevance

One of the ways to achieve relevance with Customers is with any mechanical actions you take to anticipate what Customers will use and find handy; for example, a website, a mobile site, or anything that saves them time. But the most powerful relevance factor is an emotional connection.

Remember, the buying decision has always been, and will continue to be, wholly owned by the Customer. Another thing that isn't going to change is the role the emotional component can play in a buying decision—even for B2B decisions. Never underestimate the power of emotion in your relationship with Customers.

> THIS WILL BE ON THE TEST
>
> *The customer relevance hat trick: help your Customers help their Customers help their Customers.*

Here are the two primary ways emotion impacts relevance:

1. Customers get emotional about acquiring something, like a product or service. This kind of emotion is most often experienced about something they want, especially for B2C Customers. And while likely to a lesser extent, the ownership emotion also exists for B2B Customers. You'll always want to make sure your technology is handy. But being a reliable source for Customers to get what they want—that special customization you've uncovered—is how you achieve emotional relevance with Customers.

2. Customers are also emotional about the connection they have with a Seller. All Customers have this emotion, but it is the primary one for B2B Customers, because of the reliability relationships they build with vendors and suppliers. Trust is a big part of these relationships. It has always been a powerful intangible, but there is no higher level

of trust in the B2B sector than for a Customer to let you contribute to and participate with them in serving their Customers.

Relevance, like beauty, is in the eye of the beholder. But you will never go wrong doing something for Customers that delivers a positive emotion. This was true in the Age of the Seller, and it's even more powerful in the Age of the Customer.

Chapter 16

The Rules of Selling Have Changed

Nothing happens until somebody sells something.

—Arthur H. (Red) Motley
President/Publisher
Parade Magazine (1946-1978)

There are three kinds of selling: inside sales, outside sales, and virtual sales. All three selling disciplines are being conducted successfully in the Age of the Customer but with new rules.

In chapter 6, "The Influencers," you learned how at the Moment of Relevance, Prospects use an online process of elimination to make the decision about which Seller they will buy from. For consumers, the Moment of Relevance is likely to be at or very close to the point of purchase.

For businesses, the Moment of Relevance is more complex and, consequently, we could call that process, The Journey of Relevance. On this journey there are more steps required than before, because Prospects require vendors to demonstrate their relevance before they're allowed to talk about selling.

Indeed, long before they have the chance to demonstrate how competitive they are, B2B Sellers have to receive permission to pass through what I call "The Relevance Firewall" by demonstrating most, if not all, of the following elements, which will be discussed to a greater degree later:

- Industry and solution credentials
- Accomplish some level of acquaintance
- Acquire some level of referral
- The ability to plug in at the Customer's level of understanding
- Deliver some information or collateral that demonstrates relevance and values

The goal of this chapter is to help you successfully make the transition from Age of the Seller practices, which are becoming increasingly unviable, to the new expectations of your Prospects and Customers.

Inside Sales

Inside selling is divided into two groups:

1. Salespeople who wait on Customers to visit the business, as in retail. Usually this activity is associated with business-to-consumer selling (B2C). The level of expertise for this group ranges from a part-time clerk to a professional career salesperson selling on commission. In the early part of my career, I progressed from clerk to commissioned pro.
2. Salespeople who use technology, like the telephone, to reach out to Customers to either prospect for someone to follow up later or actually close a sale with that first contact. Of course, telephone sales have been marginalized by technology, like caller ID, and by statute, like the Telemarketing and Consumer Fraud Abuse Prevention Act, which produced the National Do Not Call Registry.

> **THIS WILL BE ON THE TEST**
>
> *In the new Age, Sellers have to receive permission from Prospects to pass through their "Relevance Firewall."*

The good news is, if you're selling face-to-face in retail, essentially everything you ever needed to know to be successful still applies in the new Age. But there is one imperative of inside sales that you must follow: You have to determine what the Prospect knows. This was always a good practice, but now it is essential and must be done as soon as possible—such as when you first meet the Prospect.

As we've discussed, Customers rarely show up, or contact a Seller using technology, without having conducted some research online. In fact, there is a good chance any given Prospect knows just as much, maybe more, than any one of your salespeople. Consequently, every Seller should train their sales staff on how to use probing techniques to determine the Prospect's level of understanding, so they can plug in at the appropriate level with the right information. Otherwise, you risk annoying the Prospect by wasting their time. In the Age of the Customer, the overarching cardinal sin of any Seller is to waste a Customer's time.

Remember what we discussed in chapter 14: when any contact is made with a Prospect or Customer, regardless of the method of contact, you must include in the conversation requests to follow up with them after they leave—get permission from the Prospect to "Follow me home." This includes asking which method of contact they prefer: email, text, social media, etc. In the Age of the Customer, part of being relevant is keeping Prospects and Customers informed through the use of new communication technologies and platforms based on customer expectations.

Virtual Sales

For millennia during the Age of the Seller, and prior to the past hundred years or so, all sales contacts were made face-to-face. Either a Customer entered the establishment of a Seller, or a Seller called on a Customer at their home or establishment.

> **THIS WILL BE ON THE TEST**
>
> *In the Age of the Customer the first sales imperative is: Determine what the Prospect already knows.*

Beginning in the latter half of the 19th century, a new contact opportunity began as offerings, purchases, and deliveries were made possible through the postal service, which came to be known as doing business by "mail order." Thanks to Mr. Ward and Mr. Sears for their mail order catalogs and our first experience with virtual selling, as well as what was essentially the birth of direct mail marketing. My parents ordered my first guitar from a Montgomery Ward catalog, and I worked my way through college as a manager-in-training for Sears Roebuck and Company.

Of course, we can thank Mr. Bell for his invention, which produced a virtual variation on doing business face-to-face. Since 1877, the telephone has been the nexus we've used to conduct the various steps of doing business with Customers.

And since the advent of the Age of the Customer, Internet technologies and associated applications have created the greatest opportunities and disruptions in all of the selling disciplines, not just the virtual ones, with the e-business elements: e-shopping, e-selling, and e-customer service.

It's doubtful Ward or Sears could have imagined a day when millions of virtual catalogs would be available with the twitch of an index finger, for the purpose of shopping, comparing, purchasing, paying, and choosing a delivery method and schedule. But as we've discussed, the great disrupter is itself being disrupted as e-business moves to the next level and the latest iteration of Mr. Bell's invention. The smartphone, untethered in the palm of the hand, has become an e-business magic wand.

Outside Sales

Of the great opportunities and disruptions the Internet and associated resources have created in all aspects of the marketplace, arguably none have been more interesting than the impact on outside selling.

> **THIS WILL BE ON THE TEST**
>
> *In the Age of the Seller, salespeople were the original Internet of Prospects and Customers.*

For centuries, virtually every household and all businesses started their day knowing that they were going to be interrupted, perhaps many times, by a salesperson calling on them. Residences were called on by those selling every form of household product, machine, and gizmo. Businesses were called on by salespeople representing Sellers in the supply chain, as well as those providing administrative and operational products. For generations, B2B outside salespeople, as I was for many years, were the original Internet of their Prospects and Customers. Customers sought and received solutions from salespeople, who provided:

- Products and services
- Information about those offerings
- Information about the industry
- Technical instruction
- Experiences of other Customers
- And sometimes, persuasion

As you can see from the cartoon in Figure 8, in the Age of the Seller, businesses who were operating with outdated methods needed a salesperson to call on them to demonstrate the new tools and capability.

This kind of interruption selling was inefficient and disruptive for the Customer. But since most business was done face-to-face, for generations this was the best way to put Customers and products together.

Figure 8

The Rules of Selling Have Changed

During the Age of the Seller, getting an initial meeting was the easy step, while closing the sale was more involved and required the most skill. But Age of the Customer influences have shifted the way buyers prepare themselves to purchase products or services, from needing assistance from a salesperson, to being able to pre-qualify themselves by themselves. Buyers are avoiding prospecting calls from all but the short list of vendors they have identified as worthy in their information gathering process.

Not only has the prospecting step of the process become more time-consuming, but also more technical, with new prospect development and introduction steps being required in order for a salesperson to simply be justified in asking for a first meeting. Consequently, many sales organizations are becoming frustrated and confused, because they're experiencing a drop in qualifying meetings with Prospects, which is putting inappropriate pressure on the closing steps.

In order to relieve this frustration and confusion, and help you achieve more first meetings with Prospects, I'm going to identify how the Age of the Customer has changed the rules of outside selling, and show you how to make the necessary adjustments to be successful in this new reality.

The Two-Step Selling Process

For as long as salespeople have called on Customers, the outside selling process has been divided into what I've coined as the Two-Step Selling Process:

Step One: Get a quality, qualifying meeting in front of a decision maker.

Step Two: Qualify a Prospect and get a buying decision, hopefully in your favor.

Within these steps are the major activities required to take a Prospect from first knowledge of their existence to paying Customer.

Step One

This step is pure "shoe leather" prospecting. It has the singular purpose of identifying Suspects who may be converted into Prospects and ultimately Customers in Step Two. This step is the process of getting a Suspect to agree to schedule a first meeting where a qualifying conversation can be conducted to determine if there is a basis for doing business.

But—and this is important to understand—this step does not include the actual qualifying meeting or first call.

During the Age of the Seller, accomplishing Step One was more often about overcoming call reluctance by the salesperson than call resistance from the Prospect. In those days it wasn't very difficult to get a meeting with a decision maker, because the salesperson had the products the Prospect wanted, as well as the information the Prospect needed to make an informed decision. Indeed, it was once the norm for decision makers to spend part of their day meeting with vendors. Consequently, the greatest narrowing of the field of competitors was almost always later in the process, during Step Two.

> THIS WILL BE ON THE TEST
>
> *The Age of the Customer has changed the rules of selling.*

It became axiomatic in the marketplace that by applying the classic "shoe leather" approach, selling became a numbers game, because performance could be predicted by calculating backwards from your sales goal for any period divided by your close ratio (determined by Step Two activity). For example, if you need five sales this month and have a 50% close ratio (you sell half of the qualified Prospects you talk to), that means your Step One goal is to get in front of 10 people who can become qualified Prospects. Here's the equation:

Sales goal (5) ÷ Close ratio (50%) = Number of qualified Prospects you need (10)

This is simple math that worked like a charm for generations of sales professionals. If you failed to meet your sales goal, it might be because you didn't close enough Prospects in Step Two, but it was much more likely that you just didn't see enough people in Step One.

Step Two

This multifaceted step begins with the first qualifying meeting and includes the qualifying process, alignment of offerings with Prospect applications and expectations, delivering demonstrations and proposals, and, of course, the closing steps, including those used throughout Step Two, as well as the final closing question.

Success in Step Two requires being good at multiple selling skills ranging from conducting effective qualifying meetings, to discovering the right solution, to making a compelling competitive case, to being able to close the sale. All the while continually justifying the time granted by the Prospect.

For thousands of generations during the Age of the Seller, Step Two required salespeople to have finely honed communication, probing, presentation, selling, and closing skills, combined with extensive product and industry knowledge, both of the salesperson's industry as well as that of the Prospect.

As a result of the disparity in the degree of difficulty between Step One and Step Two, in the Age of the Seller, the sales training commitment ratio was typically 90% for Step Two and 10% for Step One. Businesses and salespeople got really good at taking a Prospect from qualifying to contract, while essentially taking Step One for granted.

THIS WILL BE ON THE TEST

In the Age of the Customer, cold calling is a fool's errand.

Age of the Customer Disruptions

As the Age of the Seller is progressively being replaced by the Age of the Customer, control is shifting, as revealed earlier, with control of two of the three main elements of any business relationship—the buying decision and easy access to the information about that decision—now being held by the Customer, leaving the product as the only element still controlled by the Seller.

But this shift in control has disrupted entrenched sales practices, methods and regimes, and perhaps none more subtly than the order of degree of difficulty of the Two-Step Selling Process. In the Age of the Customer, virtually nothing has changed in Step Two. If you're good at the multifaceted, classic sales techniques that have become tried and true for millennia, you can still close as many Prospects as ever, once you've achieved enough initial qualifying meetings.

> **THIS WILL BE ON THE TEST**
>
> *In the Age of the Customer, Prospects self-qualify themselves and pre-qualify vendors.*

The primary exception is that you will be required to quickly identify where Prospects are on their independent discovery of information regarding industry, product, application, pricing, and even customer experiences from UGC. Otherwise, you risk the chance of insulting their level of understanding and, as mentioned previously, committing arguably the Cardinal Sin of Selling—wasting a Prospect's time.

The big shift is with Step One, which has historically been taken for granted. Where this part was previously the easiest, the degree of difficulty has now inverted so that getting a quality, qualifying meeting scheduled with a Prospect has become increasingly the more difficult and complicated of the two steps. Consequently, sales organizations practicing the 90:10 ratio of training commitment for generations are seeing a decline in qualifying meetings with Prospects.

Armed with Age of the Customer resources, buyers now have access to most of the information they require to make a pre-qualifying decision. This unassisted information acquisition results in at least three disruptions to the Two-Step Selling Process:

1. A Prospect now believes, often correctly, they have enough information to essentially rule Sellers in or out before first contact is made.
2. The Age of the Seller expectation of buyers to meet with vendors as a normal course of business has been essentially relegated to only meeting with a smaller group of vendors—perhaps as few as two, or even just

one—which Prospects have, on their own, pre-qualified to meet with.

3. Prospects like this new empowerment, because it helps them get farther down the road on their decision-making journey on their own. And by reducing contact with uncompetitive vendors, it saves time and eliminates the need to tell a bunch of also-ran Sellers they're not going to get the business.

Think about the magnitude of this disruption: Where previously a Prospect was willing to be called on by salespeople to conduct the qualifying process and rule that Prospect in or out, in the Age of the Customer the Prospects themselves are:

- Increasingly self-qualifying themselves as a potential buyer.
- Prequalifying vendors prior to contact.

And here's the mother of all disruptions: All of this is often happening without the vendor knowing the Prospect even exists.

In the Age of the Seller, cold calling was a significant part of a salesperson's activity, and, because of the Seller's control of information, Customers expected to be called on face-to-face. But the cartoon in Figure 9 demonstrates what a salesperson is likely to experience in a cold-call today.

Figure 9

Businesses have to make changes to their training commitment that recognizes that the best salesperson—who will still need every Step Two skill they've ever learned and mastered—is useless if he or she cannot get in the front door to conduct enough initial qualifying meetings.

In the Age of the Customer, cold calling is a fool's errand.

New Rules, New Tools, New Attitude, New Commitment

In the Age of the Customer, every sales organization and salesperson must understand that their attitude regarding the Two-Step Selling Process must conform to the new reality. The days of taking for granted that the real work of selling begins after a Prospect is identified and the first meeting is conducted are over.

In order to achieve a high-quality first call with a Prospect, there are new rules that must be followed and new tools that must be employed prior to earning the right to ask for a first meeting. This means companies that expect their salespeople to meet sales goals now have to put as much, if not more, emphasis and resources on training, equipping, budgeting, measuring, and perhaps even compensating for the new Step One disciplines.

This list reveals new resources and behaviors that must be considered in the new Age in order for Suspects to become Prospects and then Customers.

In Figures 10 and 11 you'll see how the process has evolved from the Age of the Seller to the new Age. In both examples, the allocation of space represents the ratio of each step in the total time required to accomplish the

New Rules

- Overall selling cycle may not be longer, but the initial qualifying process is.
- Prospects self-qualify themselves *and* pre-qualify relevant vendors without help from salespeople.
- Sellers demonstrate relevance and values to Prospects before doing business.
- Self-qualified Customers have their own sense of urgency.

New Tools

- Online resources to research Prospects
- Networking—in person and online with social media
- New media—for distribution of relevant content

New Attitude

- Patience, discipline, subtle sense of urgency by salesperson
- Contribute first, contract second

New Commitment

- Recognition of, and training for, the above list of new factors

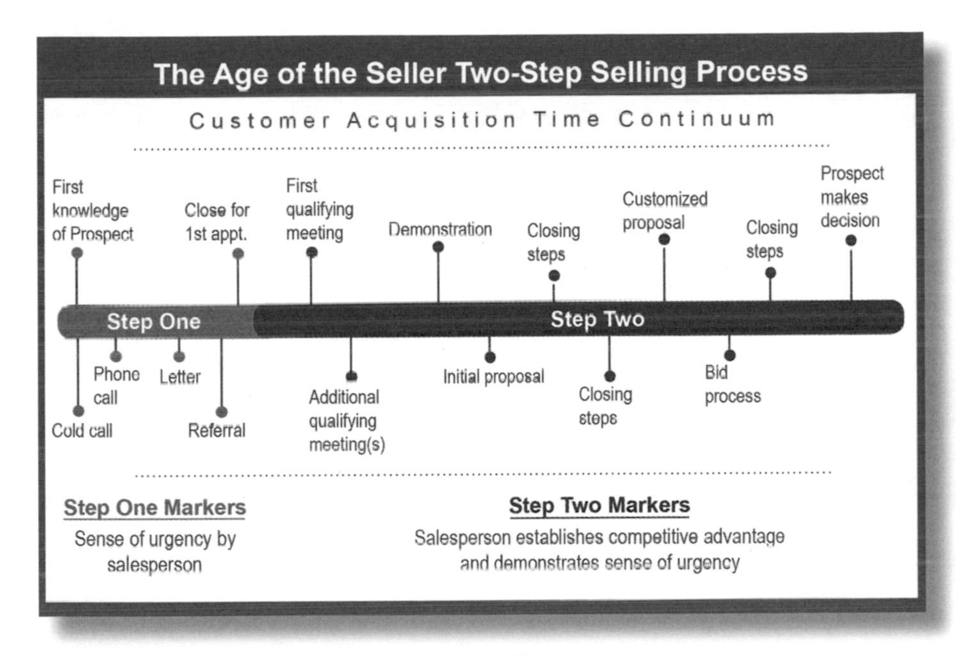

Figure 10

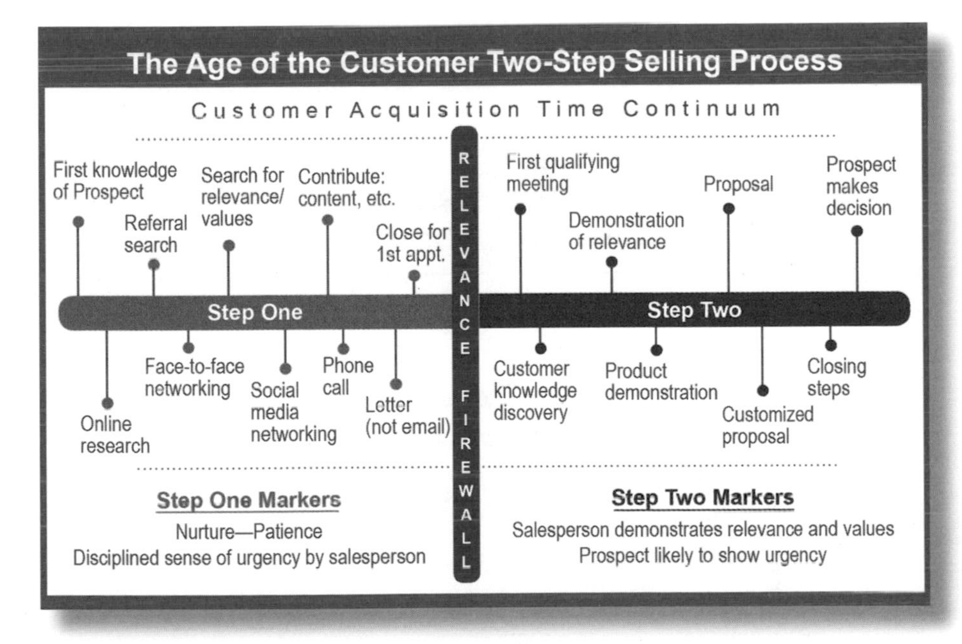

Figure 11

entire process, from initial discovery to a final decision by the Prospect. In the spirit of "a picture is worth a thousand words," just look at how the center line, which represents getting approval for the qualifying first meeting, has moved.

In the Age of the Seller continuum (Figure 10), time was heavily weighted in Step Two, since it was easier to get an initial meeting and Prospects needed a salesperson to help them more.

THIS WILL BE ON THE TEST

In the Age of the Customer, there will still be professional salespeople, but there will be fewer of them.

In the Age of the Customer continuum (Figure 11), total time of the selling cycle may not have changed, but the allocation of time for the two steps are different. Step One has become longer because more strategic activity is now required and, therefore, more time to close for a quality first meeting. Step Two is likely to be shorter since Prospects have already pre-qualified vendors during their own information gathering process, reducing the time from qualifying to closing. The good news is that self-qualified Prospects will have their own sense of urgency.

In the Age of the Customer, successful salespeople will have to be every bit as professional, skilled, and deliberate at establishing a first meeting as they ever were at closing the deal.

The Power of a Call-Back Culture

A business practice is considered systemic when it's executed throughout an organization with uniformity and regularity. And while systemic practices are beneficial to an organization, they're also often perfunctory and obligatory, which means requiring constant maintenance.

The level of desirability for any proven practice is to evolve beyond systemic to become part of the culture of an organization. When this happens, it stops being a practice and morphs into a behavior.

A business practice is executed because it's part of the system, a means to an end. But a business behavior is part of the culture, performed as a way of life. In the Age of the Customer, behaviors are what we do to demonstrate our values, sustain relevance with Customers, and achieve success for ourselves.

Regardless of everything else that's involved in the sales effort, from marketing to advertising to lead generation to virtual contact, new B2B

Customers are still most often acquired when a salesperson has face-to-face meetings with a Prospect, from the first qualifying call to follow-up meetings. However, as revealed in the previous section, it's increasingly difficult to accomplish face-to-face meetings. Consequently, the effort to achieve the maximum number of face-to-face meetings has to be more than just a systemic practice, it must become cultural behavior—a way of life.

One of the most effective sales behaviors I've ever found is as old as selling: the Call-Back Strategy. A call-back is gaining permission for a face-to-face meeting with a Prospect that has yet to commit to taking the steps in the direction of doing business. A call-back is any face-to-face meeting that happens after the initial qualifying meeting, but before the Prospect has made the buying decision. It's also used during a prolonged period of indecision by a qualified Prospect.

In the Age of the Customer, a salesperson's call-back activity must evolve from practice to behavior, and from systemic to cultural. From, "Because I was told to," to "My personal success literally depends upon it."

When a Seller accomplishes a Call-Back Culture, its sales force will continuously, effortlessly, and on their own:

- Think about how to get a face-to-face meeting with a Prospect.
- Look for and use resources and tools that are relevant to the Prospect to encourage a call-back acceptance, including articles, white papers, books, etc. Anything that—and this is the essence of the call-back strategy—can be hand-delivered.
- Execute a strategic call-back plan for each Prospect that uses resources and tools in a tactical way to move a face-to-face acceptance along at the appropriate pace for that Prospect.
- Understand that face-to-face is the original social media. And even in the new Age, where high-tech is a big part of modern customer communication options, believe that face-to-face is the ultimate high-touch and the relevance coin-of-the-realm for any B2B Prospect.

> **THIS WILL BE ON THE TEST**
>
> *One of the most effective sales behaviors is as old as selling: the Call Back.*

If you want to get more sales in the Age of the Customer, do whatever you can to achieve a Call-Back Culture. Any Seller that enjoys high employee morale and engagement due to demonstrated values and leadership should be able to skip the systemic practice stage and go directly to a successful call-back strategy as a cultural behavior.

Prepare for the Moment of Relevance

It would not be possible to address all of the ways each industry must approach executing a successful sales strategy in the new Age. But every Seller must do so with the acceptance that Customer relationships will increasingly be forged and perpetuated based on being relevant to Customers, and less on manipulative marketing strategies and sales skills. Consider ...

BLASINGAME'S LAW OF SELLING IN THE AGE OF THE CUSTOMER

Contribute first—contract second.

For generations, the classic professional salesperson called on businesses; thousands of men and women created small fortunes selling on commission in the B2B sales strata, and millions more made a very good living there. My own sales career is represented in there somewhere.

But here's a rude truth and some tough love: In the Age of the Customer, there will still be professional salespeople, but there will be fewer of them. As the original customer interface, salespeople represented the analog heroes of free market economies. But now the marketplace has new customer interfaces that are increasingly digital.

If you're looking for examples of customer interface disruptions that have already happened, look at the travel agency business and the stockbroker profession. Once the gateway to advance airline, hotel and auto rental reservations for business travelers, any surviving travel agencies are now all essentially vacation planners. Having been the keeper of the key to financial markets for individuals with an investment portfolio, surviving stockbrokers are now financial planners.

The twin pistons of the engine that's driving the Age of the Customer are disruption and opportunity. As you make plans to deal with which of these two is going to pop up first, you'll likely find the answer you're looking for hanging out near your customers' expectations, at the Moment of Relevance.

Chapter 17

Social Media: A Rose by Any Other Name

What's in a name? That which we call a rose
by any other name would smell as sweet.

—William Shakespeare
from *Romeo and Juliet*

A heretic is a true believer who doesn't like the status quo. Specifically, a heretic writes or speaks about ideas that depart from established beliefs. Here are three things we know about heretics:

1. They have the courage of their convictions. For these convictions, heretics historically have been ridiculed, ostracized, imprisoned, tortured, and even put to death.
2. Heretics are often ultimately recognized for their vision; unfortunately, usually after their death. Martin Luther was called a heretic by the 16th century Catholic Church. But today, as one of the founders of the Protestant Reformation, he's a revered historic figure.
3. A heretic is not the same thing as a contrarian. Often, a contrarian is just being contrary—a heretic is on a mission.

In my career I've often found myself playing the role of the heretic. Not for heresy's sake; it's just that when everyone else gets caught up in some frenzy or fad and doesn't understand why I'm not joining the madding crowd, it makes me slow down, look around, and ask pointed questions.

When social media really started catching on, I could feel my heretical tendencies emerging. Observing the phenomenon of the major social media platforms—Facebook, Twitter, *et al*—I began to see the good, the bad, and the ugly parts of social media. It was good that people were able to find each other, connect, and create communities. It was bad when social media became a conscious (or subconscious) substitute for actual physical interaction. And it was ugly when it became apparent that this activity had the tendency to promote narcissism and addiction. Such a scenario is heretic food.

Sometime around 2008, I started referring to myself as the "Social Media Heretic" because, while I was a true believer, I did not like the status quo assumption that the term "social" would contribute to its adoption by businesses. My new appraisal for social media determined that as handy as the term was for individuals, social media was unfortunately unintuitive to most business owners and managers.

Nevertheless, I declared many times on my radio program and wrote more than once in my column that, while social media was definitely a craze, it was not a fad; it was not going away. My prediction was that once the mania had subsided, like everything else that has intrinsic value, social media would become a ubiquitous tool, perhaps even a utility, much like the telephone. And remember, if my prediction comes to pass, that will be good news for the builders of Community, but not necessarily for any particular social media platform.

THIS WILL BE ON THE TEST

A contrarian is just being contrary— a heretic is on a mission.

But the above appraisal was for individuals. And since my work is focused on businesses, I began observing that while social media was intuitive and fall-off-a-log easy for individuals, it just wasn't catching on among small businesses. To find out why, we began polling small business owners about their social media activity: Are you doing it? Do you have a strategy? Is it working? Where are you stuck? The responses we received were not encouraging for the adoption of social media by small firms.

This chapter is not intended to help you with the details of executing a social media strategy for your business. There are many very competent and smart people helping small businesses develop and execute a social media strategy through their writing and consulting work, and I recommend you take advantage of their expertise. This chapter is to help you put social media for your business in the proper perspective, and to focus on the challenge many small businesses have making the commitment to invest time and resources in something that is so unlike anything they've ever done before.

A Rose by Any Other Name

The default goal of every Seller is to be financially successful. Investments of time, energy, and capital are made to find, qualify, and convert Prospects into Customers and, ultimately, that sales revenue into the mother's milk of the marketplace—profits. And as with every investment plan, the ROI questions are imperative: What is the return? When will it happen? Consequently, it has become obvious that too many small businesses have been running into at least three stumbling blocks as they've tried to marry the ROI imperative with executing a social media strategy:

- What does "social" have to do with doing business?
- Social media activity is not like anything else a business does.
- Identifying return on investment—even if it's just time—in a social media strategy requires more commitment and patience than most other investments.

When a manager thinks about market activity, he or she thinks about meeting a Prospect in the marketplace where everyone knows why they are there, which is to buy and sell. But in the social media marketplace—where Sellers are involved—the rules are different. Let me say that another way: Selling in the social media marketplace is different from selling in the traditional marketplace.

The singular distinction of social media activity is that it builds Community. Consequently, I started recommending that when business owners evaluate an investment in a social media strategy, they use the term *online customer Communities* or *building online customer Communities*, because in the marketplace that's what social media does.

BLASINGAME'S LAWS OF SMALL BUSINESS SOCIAL MEDIA

1. *Your goal is to build online customer Communities.*
2. *Your prime directive is "Contribute first, contract second."*
3. *Your future Customers will increasingly come from Community-building activity and less from Age of the Seller marketing practices and prospect development activity.*

Unlike traditional advertising, with the obligatory call-to-action to motivate Prospects to buy now, paying for the placement of your brand in a strategic location is a long-view marketing and brand-building decision. Developing and investing in an online customer community building strategy requires a similar attitude and level of patience that is required in making a brand-building investment. For more on what this level of patience looks like, see the Communities section in chapter 6, "The Influencers."

Beware the Major Social Media Platforms

Another reason for my social media heresy is skepticism of the long-term behavior of the major social media platforms. I encourage business owners to use Facebook, Twitter, and other platforms as a training ground for their teams. I encourage them to learn how the social marketplace is different from the traditional marketplace and to find, engage, and develop relationships with Prospects and Customers. But all the while I also tell them not to completely trust these platforms.

There aren't too many things more important to your business's future than your prospect and customer lists. And since you should think of your social media strategy as building online customer Communities, it follows that the members of the Communities you build and join online qualify to be on those lists. But how you get them transferred from an online Community to a prospect and customer list is part of those new rules I mentioned earlier.

So here's the heretic question: What happens to all of the work you've done to build and join online customer Communities, and what happens to all those community contacts if Facebook, for example, just goes away? Sure this isn't likely, but it could happen. It has happened. Maybe not just disappear, but what if they changed the rules? What if they change how they do business in such a way that it disrupts the connection between you and your Community? If you're already using the big platforms, you should be nodding your head in agreement with me, because you've already experienced how they make changes all the time without consulting their Users.

> **THIS WILL BE ON THE TEST**
>
> *For Sellers, social media is building online customer Communities.*

If you think this can't happen, just remember that Facebook and many of the large platforms are publicly-traded companies. That means they dance to the tune of only one player, and it's not their Users or even their advertising

Customers. They are 100% beholden to Wall Street, which is 100% beholden to the share price. So if driving the share price requires making adjustments in a large platform's user interface, that changes the rules of how you work with your Communities. Share price wins and you lose.

So how do you take advantage of the community-building resources available from the large platforms while minimizing the potential loss of access to your online customer Communities? The answer is one word and it's what ducks do: migrate. When you create a connection on Facebook, Twitter, etc., as soon as is reasonable (remember how I described the tone and patience of your Community activity in chapter 7, "Value and Values"?) get contact information and migrate those contacts over to a platform you have control over, like an email list. This isn't either/or, it's both/and. Unlike the Age of the Seller customer lists mentioned earlier, where you just have one place to put a name, in the Age of the Customer you will manage parallel universes of customer community contacts and:

> **THIS WILL BE ON THE TEST**
>
> *Large social media platforms are 100% beholden to Wall Street—not to you.*

- Develop Prospects and Customers through the online Communities you join and build on someone else's platform.
- As soon as you can, migrate online Community contacts to a platform or list you control.

Building online customer Communities is a very powerful Age of the Customer activity in which every business must be engaged. Here is a review of my Social Media Heretic recommendations of things you should do simultaneously with executing your classic and essential business model of engaging and selling Customers.

- Understand that for your business, social media means building online customer Communities.
- Recognize that the rules of engagement for Community building are different from selling.
- Develop the discipline and patience to execute the Community-building rules of engagement, which is "contribute first, contract second."
- Think of your Community-building strategy ROI as more of an investment in your business's future and less as a call-to-action strategy.

- Join and create online customer Communities that align with your business model.
- Use the large platforms—Facebook, Twitter, LinkedIn, etc.—as training grounds for you and your team.
- Use the large platforms to gain access to diverse Communities to which you otherwise would not have access.
- Minimize exposure to the motivations of the large platforms by migrating Community contacts over to your own platforms so that they exist in parallel contact universes.

Developing and executing a social media strategy is a marathon race. And here's the good news for small business: You don't have to win this race to be successful. But in order to avoid being subducted, you do have to participate, and it will help if you can at least keep the leaders in sight.

In the Age of the Customer, building online customer Communities has become a business practice imperative.

Prepare for the Moment of Relevance

Decades ago, prior to my career with Xerox, I was already a seasoned professional trainer and salesperson: My years with Sears and the U.S. Army had already taught me a lot about communicating and influencing others. But when Xerox hired me as a salesperson, they sent me to their national school and provided what was in my opinion the most powerful selling skills program ever, Professional Selling Skills (PSS).

In the session on closing, the instruction included a set of 13 different closes. These were communication skills that helped to convert whatever you and the Prospect were talking about into an opportunity to ask for the business—to close the sale. One day the instructor went around the room and asked each of us how many closes we thought they were comfortable using. Some of my classmates were newer to sales and admitted that they felt confident in two closes, or maybe three.

> **THIS WILL BE ON THE TEST**
>
> *You don't have to win the social media race, but you do have to participate.*

When the time came for my answer, I sincerely thought about it and said, "I don't know." The instructor replied that was, in fact, the right answer. She meant that we should become so fluent and accomplished with the closing techniques that they were seamlessly integrated into our selling activity.

Certain markers will identify when the Age of the Seller has been fully subducted by the Age of the Customer. One of those markers is when we no longer think about, talk about, or worry about having a social media or online community building strategy. That's because what we have been executing as a separate strategy will then be seamlessly integrated into all of our other customer acquisition activity: brand building, marketing, advertising, prospect identification, prospect development, converting Prospects into Customers, serving Customers, and maintaining those relationships.

And when all of this comes to pass, achieving customer relevance will also become seamless.

People are hungry for stories. It's part of our very being.

—Studs Terkel

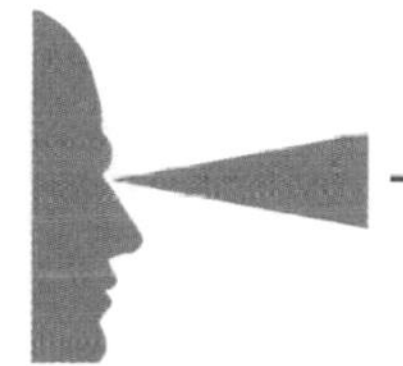

Chapter 18

The Power of Stories

Sellers who will be the most successful in the Age of the Customer are those who most effectively use the newest human developments to tap into one of the oldest traits of humanity. Allow me to explain why this is important and how to accomplish it by telling a few stories.

Cogito Ergo Sum

In 1637, Rene Descartes, recognized as the father of western philosophy, wrote this thought, "*Cogito ergo sum*," from his work *Discourse on the Method*. In English it translates to, "I think, therefore I am." Certainly the power of abstract thought is what separates you and me from other members of the kingdom Animalia.

But if Descartes had had the benefit of recent research, he might have modified his philosophy. Anthropologists now believe Homo sapiens succeeded, unlike other members of the genus Homo, Neanderthals, and Cro-Magnon for example, because our brains had a greater capacity for speech and language. Today Descartes might update his philosophy to "I think and speak, therefore I am."

If asked to name the most important primordial development of humankind, you would probably feel quite confident in saying the harnessing of fire or the invention of the wheel. Indeed, both important human developments. But perhaps the most important existential human trait is the ability to tell stories.

In *The Wealth of Nations*, Adam Smith identified the written word as one of the three great human inventions. But long before humans invented writing, we were telling stories. And these stories—told, memorized, and retold over millennia—became the headwaters of human development.

Storytelling: Your Past

Another thing that's older than the written word is the marketplace. Long before ad copy, Sellers were verbalizing the value and benefits of their wares.

And surely this early storytelling was the origin of modern sales skills.

As a pup salesman I was trained to practice a list of different kinds of closes—verbal techniques to use to close a sale. As I mentioned in the last chapter, there were thirteen of these, including the Puppy Dog Close, the Sharp Angle Close, and the Alternative Close, just to name a few. But the one that I always felt was the most powerful was the Similar Situation Close.

The Similar Situation Close is used when a Prospect is almost ready to buy, but they can't quite pull the trigger. Usually, they just need to feel more confident about the decision, which is when I would tell a story about one of my customers who found themselves in a "similar situation." The story would usually be about real people and experiences that were, in fact, similar to this prospect's situation, but sometimes it would be a composite of different customers, possibly with a touch of similar situation license. This storytelling sales technique produced a lot of sales for me over the years.

THIS WILL BE ON THE TEST

Long before advertisement, Sellers were telling stories about the value and benefits of their wares.

The reason the Similar Situation Close is arguably the most powerful of all closes is because its active ingredient is the primordial attraction humans have to the telling of a story. And we love to listen to stories perhaps almost as much as we love to tell them.

Storytelling: Two Prophets Predict Your Future

In the mid 1960s, Intel's co-founder Gordon Moore proposed what is now called "Moore's Law," which, over the intervening years has become, "The processing power of computers will double every two years." Indeed, since Moore's initial observation, technological capability has compounded pretty much at this pace. But as Moore's Law has played out, it has manifested in three developments that are key components of the shift from the Age of the Seller to the Age of the Customer:

1. As processing power increased, form factors became increasingly smaller, as room-size computers morphed into smartphones.
2. Barriers to access of information were lowered as analog hard copy became digital web pages.
3. New media tools have given virtually every Earthling the ability to

produce and distribute stories, potentially to every other human on the planet.

In his 1982 watershed book, *Megatrends*, futurist John Naisbitt offered this idea: "The more we adopt high tech, the more we will want high touch." Now no less than a prophecy, we continue to see evidence of how high-tech innovations are almost always beholden to an expectation of high touch by adopters: Consider that at the heart of most current innovations is a connectivity and Community component.

So not long after one prophet told us that our technological capability would double every two years, the second prophet told us that not only would all this digital development not supplant our primal human need for Community, it would actually intensify it.

Storytelling: Your Future

Storytelling is humanity spoken. In the marketplace, small businesses are the face and voice of humanity, which provides them with a great advantage in the Age of the Customer. No sector of the marketplace can be as effective telling stories as a small business. And whether these stories are delivered in person or published for multimedia distribution, they should conform to …

BLASINGAME'S 4 Cs OF STORYTELLING

1. Connect *to Prospects on an emotional level with a story.*
2. Convey *your expertise, humanity, values, and relevance with a story.*
3. Create *a memory with a story that a Customer will always associate with you.*
4. Convert *Prospects into Customers with the use of stories.*

When people assemble in Communities, they tell stories. When Prospects discuss and learn about the values of a person or Seller, it's often from a story. These high-touch activities have become the customer acquisition coins of the realm in the Age of the Customer, and all are strengthened with stories.

In the Age of the Customer, as you have learned, relevance trumps competitiveness. In this new Age there are two ways to deliver a story that meets a Prospect's relevance expectations: face-to-face and publishing, which we'll talk about in the next chapter. Regardless of the delivery method, these stories should be about:

- How to use your products to achieve the most value
- Similar situations of other Customers
- Activities in, and support of, the Community
- Organizational accomplishments
- Your employees' accomplishments
- Your company
- Yourself
- (Your idea here)

There is one level of excellence above being a good and consistent storyteller: when your story is so compelling that someone else re-tells or distributes your story, or their own positive story about you and your business. In the "Customer Expectations" section of chapter 12, I identified this as "earned media," and it's the pinnacle of storytelling and the Holy Grail of marketing in the Age of the Customer.

> **THIS WILL BE ON THE TEST**
>
> *Grow your business with minimum expense and maximum impact—tell more stories.*

Prepare for the Moment of Relevance

Sellers who will be the most successful in the Age of the Customer are those who effectively tap into one of the oldest traits of humanity by engaging Prospects and Customers with stories. They will either deliver these stories in person or publish them for multimedia distribution, but either way they will tell stories as a way of life, not just as a means to an end.

The best way to tell a story hasn't changed in the new Age. Face-to-face is the original social media and is still the most powerful, tried and true storytelling delivery method. But face-to-face has limited capability to leverage your stories, which is why every small business has to become a publisher—a publisher of marketing messages and customer resources, and a publisher of stories. We'll talk about this more in the next chapter.

Finally, answer this question: How much does it cost to harness the power of a story? Exactly! If you want to grow your business with minimum expense and maximum impact, tell stories. Tell lots of stories.

Too many brands treat social media as a one way, broadcast channel, rather than a two-way dialogue through which emotional storytelling can be transferred.

—Simon Mainwaring

Chapter 19

You Must Become a Publisher

> *I finished my first book seventy-six years ago and offered it to every publisher on earth. Their refusals were unanimous: and it did not get into print until fifty years later, when publishers would publish anything that had my name on it.*
>
> —George Bernard Shaw

Even though writing is, according to Adam Smith, one of the three great human inventions, as late as the 15th century no constituency existed for the published word, because most people were illiterate. But that all changed around 1450 when Johannes Gutenberg's invention of the printing press with moveable type produced the first Gutenberg Bible. Over the next half-century 20 million books were published, which might not seem like a lot until you realize that at the time, Europe had an estimated population of 57 million potential book customers. Clearly, publishing's time had come.

Publishing is the process of producing and distributing content: ideas, information, entertainment, and other intellectual property. A publisher possesses the skills, organization, assets, connections, and channels required to essentially manufacture content into a marketable form and then distribute it to a network of channels that ultimately lead to the consumer of what has been published. Between Gutenberg and 1993, examples of traditional publishing sectors included: books, music, newspapers, magazines, broadcast radio, and television networks.

As it has always been, ideas come from individuals. But for hundreds of years, for an individual's ideas to be distributed to any significant degree they had to be accepted, assembled, edited, and manufactured into a distributable form by a publisher in one of the media industry sectors. Publishers had the infrastructure and, more importantly, channels to the audience that authors needed to reach. Consequently, publishers held essentially an impenetrable position as gatekeepers to the public, which is to say, the paying customer and the business model for authors of any intellectual property: words, music, design, etc.

But as you will see, the concept of publishing has taken on a much more decentralized and democratic form. In the Age of the Customer, if you regularly document your personal ideas and/or business information on a blog, for example, you're a publisher. If you video yourself showing Customers how to safely remove, sharpen, and replace the blade on one of the lawn mowers you sell, post that video on YouTube or Vimeo, and/or embed it on your website or blog, you just published digital information.

If you observe traditional publishers, they have a publishing schedule. Their Customers expect them to deliver their product often and on time. That's why I think the *regular* component is critical to the definition—to be a publisher presumes there is an audience with expectations of content distribution continuity. And to show you I practice what I preach, I became a publisher on November 14, 1999, when I published and distributed my first e-zine, *The Small Business Advocate® NEWSLETTER*, and I have not missed a Sunday deadline since.

The Shift in Publishing Paradigms

The beginning of the end of iron fist control by traditional publishers happened in 1993, when the Internet was made available to the public for the first time, the web browser Mosaic was introduced, and the Age of the Customer was born.

> **THIS WILL BE ON THE TEST**
>
> *Every opportunity created by innovation also produces a disruption.*

In the Age of the Seller, publishers were powerful. But for the past generation, Age of the Customer innovations have digitized and democratized the ability to publish, resulting in no less than a classic paradigm shift in the publishing industry.

Sir Isaac Newton would be happy to know that his Third Law of Motion—for every action there is an equal and opposite reaction—is alive and well in the marketplace. For essentially every opportunity created by an Age of the Customer innovation, a disruption is also produced. Consider these publishing paradigm shift examples:

The Publishing Paradigm Shift

Age of the Seller		Age of the Customer
Newsstand, bookstore, etc.	→	Internet, web browser, email
Newspapers and magazines	→	Websites and blogs
Physical music media	→	Digital music, iTunes, etc.
Book publishers	→	Self-publishing and e-books
Physical distribution	→	Digital media
Television and radio	→	Videos, podcasts, social media, etc.
Commercial messages	→	Remote control, DVR, TiVo, etc.

Notice the common denominator of the right column—digital. Indeed, the future of publishing is digital—creation, delivery, and consumption. And while this is not good news for traditional publishers, who have previously controlled their industry with analog and physical products, it's good news for the new Age of the Customer publishers, small businesses.

If you're in any of the publishing sectors in the left column, you don't have to be told how much your world has been disrupted—perhaps even destroyed. Few industries have been impacted more dramatically by the new Age than the traditional publishing industry.

Content Is King

One of the most often invoked Internet maxims, probably originating around 1999, is "Content is King." The context of this generally accepted truth is that technology and networks were going to become little more than utilities, while one of the major creators of relevance is content—your content.

So what does all of this mean for a small business owner? It's simple: If you want to be relevant in the Age of the Customer, you have to produce and publish more content. And the good news for small businesses is that new technology, digital publishing platforms, and distribution channels make it easy and affordable to do—and it's getting easier to customize.

You Can—and Must—Become a Publisher

Remember this definition of a publisher? One who possesses the skills, organization, assets, connections, and channels required to essentially manufacture content into a marketable form and then distribute it to a network of channels, ultimately leading to the consumer.

Now, let's break this definition down and talk about how the Age of the Customer not only has made it possible for you to become a publisher, but actually requires it. The active ingredients that gave publishers control of this industry for hundreds of years include:

- *Skills:* content acquisition, editing, artists, etc.
- *Assets:* significant capital, equipment, and analog technology
- *Connections and Communities:* network of like-minded parties
- *Channels of distribution:* wholesalers, retailers, affiliates, subscribers
- *Ideas, content, intellectual property, etc.:* acquired from authors by contract
- *Marketable form:* manufacture content into a physical product
- *Organization:* significant and skilled staff to perform the above tasks

Now, let's take these elements and apply them as they're found in the Age of the Customer:

Publishing Elements in the Age of the Customer

Skills	
Content acquisition, editing, artists, etc.	It's your content. You can accomplish basic publishing skills, especially with digital technology, and hire strategic freelance professionals if you need them.
Assets	
Equipment and technology	You can afford to acquire and learn to use the same digital technology that traditional publishers use today.
Connections and Communities	
Network of like-minded parties	Use the power of the Internet with paid and natural search marketing, plus social media platforms, to join and create Communities that are consumers of your content.

→

Channels of Distribution	
Subscribers, outlets, affiliates	You can create a website, ezine, blog, YouTube channel (Vimeo, etc.), etc. on which you publish the written, audio, and video content you produce.
Ideas, Content, Intellectual Property, Etc.	
Acquired from authors	You already have the ideas and information because you're the author.
Marketable Form	
Turn content into a successful product	You can hire this skill if you need a highly produced product, but in the Age of the Customer, consumers of information are less interested in form and more interested in access to the content.
Organization	
Requires significant personnel to perform the above tasks	You don't need an expensive and elaborate organizational chart to get your message in front of consumers of your ideas—your Customers.

Pay Attention to User Interfaces

Today you have powerful publishing technology literally at your fingertips that would have seemed like magic or science fiction barely a generation ago. But regardless of the publishing tools used, the relevance of your content could be compromised by what Customers have to do to consume what you publish. And in this case, relevance will be measured by the intuitive and helpful nature of the user interface of your technology—what your digital presentation looks like to Users, Prospects, and Customers, and what they have to do to use it.

In a conversation with an EVP of marketing at a global company that serves millions of small businesses, she told me she had just gone on their website to sign up for one of their offerings. She was shocked at how frustrated she got with her own customer interface. So here are some questions to answer:

- Have you used your own digital offerings?
- Do you receive your own electronic distributions to make sure your emails, texts, etc. are delivered in a way that promotes their use by a recipient?
- How much information do you require in order to subscribe to something you offer, like a newsletter? Less is always better.
- How many clicks does someone have to make in order to read your articles, listen to a podcast, or view a video? Fewer is always better.
- When a visitor follows your content to the end, do you help them get back to a place that's handy for them?

To help you think about this, consider …

BLASINGAME'S LAW OF USER INTERFACES

Never ask a Customer to use your technology unless it's fall-off-a-log easy.

Keep new technology in the development stage until your best Customers have given it their seal of approval. And don't ask anyone to use your technology or subscribe to and receive your digital resources, unless it passes your own frustration and irritation test.

Then, and only then, will it pass the Moment of Relevance test.

An Age of the Customer Publishing Story

Allow me to tell you the story about how I started and grew as a publisher by taking advantage of all of the Age of the Customer tools and resources I've mentioned so far.

Even though I consider public access to the Internet in 1993 as the launch date of the Age of the Customer, it must be noted that the device we've always used to access the Internet is a computer of some sort. Clearly the invention, availability, and proliferation of the personal computer beginning in the late 1970s became an essential foundation for the new Age. Also software programs created in the 1980s for PCs (especially Macintosh) set millions on the path toward content creation and automation, which is the essence of publishing.

My first real understanding of the potential power of the democratization of publishing was when I purchased PageMaker 1.0 in the mid-1980s for my Mac SE. This program allowed me to turn plain text into a stylized published product. Indeed, years later, my first book was laid out in PageMaker 7.0 and delivered to the printer exactly as the big publishing houses delivered their books to their printers.

A New Media Company

In October 1997 I founded Small Business Network, Inc. as a media company. Our first offering was our website, SmallBusinessAdvocate.com. On November 17, 1997, I began my nationally syndicated radio program, The Small Business Advocate Show, and every weekday since I've produced and conducted two hours of small business content. My show initially was launched as a radio broadcast, but we soon added an Internet simulcast in January 1998.

> **THIS WILL BE ON THE TEST**
>
> *Age of the Customer innovations have digitized and democratized your ability to publish.*

By 1999 we really increased our publishing activity with two new elements: 1) we recorded each of my radio interviews and then edited them into what are now thousands of podcasts available from my website; 2) we launched the e-zine in order to distribute my small business articles using email software to publish and distribute it to an opt-in email list of subscribers.

A Publisher of Books

One of the things I get to do on my talk show is interview authors. I've done this thousands of times since 1997 and almost always ask about the relationship with their publisher, if they had one. I'm sorry to report that the comments were 10:1 negative to positive.

Based on the feedback just mentioned, and because of our organization, my experience, business background, media platform and, yes, because I might be just a tiny bit of a control freak, in 2002 we founded SBN Books to publish my books. This was our reasoning:

- We had the essential tools available to us that any big publisher had.
- We were able to acquire the resources we didn't have.
- We didn't want to wait on the approval and schedule of a big publisher.

- We didn't want to lose control of our property.
- We didn't want to split the money with a partner that didn't bring anything to the table we didn't already have.
- And there's that tiny control freak thing.

"Vanity Press" is an old pejorative used to describe people who printed their own book when they couldn't get their book anointed as worthy by one of the big publishers. One of the markers of a Vanity Press author is a basement or garage full of unsold books.

"Self-published" is the term I apply to any author who's willing to do the work of getting their book written and in a consumable form for readers, plus one more imperative: They have to have a plan to get their book in the hands of readers. That's the difference between Vanity Press and Self-Published—a successful marketing plan.

It's been told to me by industry experts that the average business book published by big publishers sells about 5,000 books. As of this writing, SBN Books has sold over 120,000 copies of my first three books. A big New York publisher once tried to ridicule me with, as she put it, "I guess you can keep selling books out the back door." I told her, "My books may go out the back door, but the checks come in the front door and I don't have to split them with you."

My publishing guru is Dan Poynter, author of *Dan Poynter's Self-Publishing Manual*, the bible on self-publishing, who taught me how to think about marketing my books. And one of my original Brain Trust members, Russell Brown, helped me understand the financial elements of self-publishing. Since then I've helped dozens of authors make the decision whether or not to self-publish. But let me hasten to add, self-publishing is not for everyone.

THIS WILL BE ON THE TEST

The difference between Vanity Press and Self-Publishing is a successful marketing plan.

We continue to publish and distribute content I create from my radio interviews, articles written by me and my Brain Trust, ultimately adding a knowledgebase, AskJim.biz, my blog, JimsBlog.biz, a Facebook Fan Page, Twitter account, e-books, and YouTube and Vimeo channels for our newest media form, videos. We also created a mobile version of our website.

With the exception of the hardback version of my books, all elements of our publishing activity is created and distributed digitally, which is the only way my small business could have accomplished what we have.

You Can Do Everything I Did

The reason I wanted to tell you about my publishing career is that there is *nothing* I did that you can't do. You don't need a lot of capital—I was broke when I started. You don't have to have a lot of experience—the tools made us look like we did. You don't have to have great contacts—we didn't either at first, but we do now.

> **THIS WILL BE ON THE TEST**
>
> *Online content should be relevant, real, short, regular, and form follows function.*

You don't have to start a radio program or write a book or become a columnist to become a publisher. Regardless of what you do or sell, there are Prospects and Customers who are looking for useful content from regular small businesses just like yours. The expectations of most consumers of information in the Age of the Customer are:

- *Relevant*—to them
- *Real*—meaning human
- *Short*—long attention spans are victims of the new Age
- *Regular*—weekly, monthly, quarterly, seasonal
- *Form follows function*—many people today would rather have all of the above, especially the frequency, than a time-consuming, highly produced version.

In Your Own Words

Long before there were blogs—at least since 1999—two of the many things I've encouraged small business owners to do is: 1) develop better writing skills; 2) whether they're yours or not, publish more words online that communicate and connect with Customers.

There was a time—before 1993—when Sellers and Customers didn't really have much of a dialogue. Customers needed to buy stuff, Sellers needed to sell stuff, and any communicating was mostly about the stuff. The Age of the Customer, with all of its associated innovations, including the Internet, email, e-commerce, social media, etc., has empowered Customers with a new platform from which they can learn and seek answers about your stuff long before you ever hear their voice, see their face, or even know they exist.

One might leap to the conclusion that increased demand for digital content would translate into more professional writing—and to some degree this is true. When it comes to website copy, artful language, proper grammar, punctuation, etc., are definitely important. But that's not dialogue. Today, after consuming information and marketing messages on your website, ads, and/or brochures, Customers are finding a growing appetite for dialogue with the Sellers they do business with. And people don't have dialogue with machines or websites; they have it with real people speaking and writing conversationally. Why do you think social media has become such a written word phenomenon?

THIS WILL BE ON THE TEST

Regardless of what you sell, Prospects and Customers are looking for information from you.

In the new Age, your Customers want to read or hear about your stuff just to make sure you actually sell what they want, but they also want to have access to real words directly from the humans behind the business. Not marketing messages, but straight-from-the-horse's-mouth words to deliver something that is increasingly a big deal to Customers: the values of the people behind the stuff. And that message has to be delivered by the humans, as unartful and unscripted as they may be.

So don't worry that you're not a professional wordsmith. When you need that kind of content, hire it done. But you do want to work on getting more comfortable with establishing a record of your own real-world, authentic words—whether physical or digital—so you can convey to Prospects and Customers your values and vision for how you want to serve them. You may also find that this exercise will help you communicate more effectively with employees and vendors.

Of course, you'll still use marketing to help Prospects find you the first time. But increasingly, Customers want to be treated more like insiders than the general public. This means initiating the dialogue—in your own words—with Customers. And here's a bonus that can pay big dividends: When the dialogue you have with Customers is recorded online, like in a blog, on a website, or one of the social media platforms, Users and Prospects can also find it. And that sets the stage for an attraction that can happen before you know they exist.

Prepare for the Moment of Relevance

Customers want to know what you think and what you know. They will read the words you publish on Twitter, Facebook or LinkedIn. They will see the thoughts you publish on your website and on your blog. They will listen to your words on a podcast that you publish on your website. They will watch a 90-second video you produce with a webcam or your smartphone, publish on YouTube or Vimeo, and then link back to your website.

When you do any or all of these things, especially on a regular basis, you're a publisher: You created and produced ideas and information and distributed it to Customers. And remember, just as small businesses don't have to conquer the world to be successful, the way the Big Box Businesses have to, you don't have to conquer the publishing world, either. You just need to reach those people who are interested in what you have to say and what you have to sell.

Publishing is now, and will increasingly be a relevance benchmark for the people you want to reach and convert into Customers. Publish and deliver what you know to Prospects and Customers in some form of media.

Just get started—like I did. You can do it.

Intellectual property, more than ever, is a line drawn around information, which asserts that despite having been set loose in the world—and having, inevitably, been created out of an individual's relationship with the world—that information retains some connection with its author that allows that person some control over how it is replicated and used.

—Nick Harkaway
Author, *The Blind Giant*

Chapter 20

The Power Twins: Innovation & IP

He who receives an idea from me, receives instruction himself without lessening mine; as he who lights his wick at mine, receives light without darkening me.

—Thomas Jefferson

Intellectual property (IP) is, by definition, the product of someone's creativity and innovation. Major categories and examples include:

- *Copyright:* The melody or words of a song; a poem; an idea expressed in words, like an article or a book; and digital IP, like software. You only need to prove yourself the creator or the legal owner to claim and protect a copyright, but a Library of Congress registration would be best.
- *Trademark:* A company logo; a title or slogan; a product name, etc. After you receive approval and permission from the government Patent and Trademark Office you can affix the ® by a mark. Until then, use the trademark, TM, or service mark, SM.
- *Patent:* An inventor is granted property rights of a unique product or process by the government Patent Office.
- *Trade secrets:* Your ideas, inventions, and processes that you create or own and that add value to your business. But rather than make them public, like with a patent, you make the decision to not reveal the details of the trade secret asset to the public. Think of the formula for Coca-Cola or KFC's chicken with "11 different herbs and spices."

This list is not meant to represent legal definitions. It's meant to represent, in lay terms, the world of IP, a.k.a. intangible assets. Also, when I use the term IP here, it means both intangible assets that you can acquire, as well as the kind that you create. In the Age of the Customer, it's difficult to talk about one without the other. For example, many small business owners have gotten rich developing and selling their own IP that they built on the Windows platforms, which is Microsoft's IP. Either way, IP is the intangible assets that you employ to execute your goals.

The Evolution of Business Assets

One of the most interesting aspects of the Age of the Customer is how it's impacting the evolution of business assets and how they're used. For most of history, business leverage came from any combination of the following three basic categories, in order of chronological appearance:

1. Muscle power (human or animal)
2. Tangible stuff (raw material, buildings, inventory, machines, etc.)
3. Intangible stuff (information, patents, trademarks, and other intellectual property or IP)

In the Age of the Seller, first the strongest caveman and biggest horses had the advantage. Then it was the fastest ships and the largest factories gaining an advantage over lesser competitors. For a small business in the latter days of the original Age, it sounded like this: "We have the largest inventory in the area."

During most of the Age of the Seller, business assets were heavily weighted in the first two categories. But, as proven by one of my Brain Trust members, Kenneth Krosin, now a retired IP attorney, all of this was changing. (We used to call IP attorneys patent attorneys, but today IP is a much more comprehensive term that better describes the growing array of intangible assets being created and used by all participants in the Age of the Customer.)

THIS WILL BE ON THE TEST

Tangible assets we acquire in the future will be determined by IP innovations.

At the end of the 20th century, Krosin conducted a study of the evolution of assets corporations owned and used to accomplish their current goals and prepare for the future during a 30-year period from the late 1970s to the late 1990s. Here's the key finding of his work:

At the beginning of the period studied, corporate assets on balance sheets were represented by 80% tangible—such as buildings, equipment, etc., and

20% intangible—like patents, trademarks, technology, etc. By the end of the period, the ratio of assets had essentially inverted to 73% intangible and the rest tangible. Considering how many centuries the original 80:20 ratio had held, to have the two major asset classes essentially invert over a 30-year period is nothing short of a balance sheet whiplash. No doubt much of this shift was heavily influenced by the Internet and digital explosion that happened during the last part of the study period in the 1990s.

The Krosin study first came to my attention around 2002. The breathtaking inversion of asset classes it revealed produced a moment of clarity: The exciting and dramatic Internet resources and other digital innovations were converging and coalescing in front of our eyes to make intangible assets, as a class, a much greater lever for businesses of all sizes. Plus, 2002 was a time when intangible, Internet-related resources were shifting from two-dimensional, information-sharing websites to tools and solutions that were creating a new virtual marketplace where Sellers and Customers could do business in Cyber Street, as well as Main Street and Wall Street.

THIS WILL BE ON THE TEST

Small businesses must acquire and create IP as a strategy to grow and sustain success.

Intellectual property, for centuries little more than a marginal marketplace advantage even for big business, is becoming the two-edged sword of opportunity and disruption in the new Age: opportunity for those who have a strategy for leveraging intangible assets more and tangible less, disruption for those who do not.

With a generation of micro-processing behind us and the Internet universe exploding around us, it became clear to me that I had to focus more of my work on helping small businesses claim what was no longer the franchise of big businesses: create and adopt IP as a strategy to grow and sustain success. In time, this perspective would help me connect the dots that revealed the transition Sellers have to make from being merely competitive to Customers to being relevant to them.

Two IP Stories

This story supports Krosin's research:

Not that long ago, I met a man who was the manager of a paper mill owned by an international corporation. This plant makes "brown" paper, which is almost every paper product you use—paper towels, napkins, etc.—as opposed to "fine" paper, like printing stock. His job was to build plants like this one from bare earth, a "green field project," get it up and running at full operating capacity, and then hand it over to a resident general manager.

When I asked him how many of the employees at his plant used computers in the direct performance of their jobs, he said, "100%." Then I asked how many employees were needed to operate this new factory. He said, "Four hundred—half as many as the same plant I built 10 years ago."

This company produces a commodity—not something high-tech—and was able to reduce its payroll by half over a 10-year period at its new facility. Imagine how different the economic impact was for the supply chain and local marketplace where this new, high-tech plant was built, compared to that of the older plant. Think about the opportunities and disruptions IP created for that local economy.

Here's another example:

In the latter half of the period Krosin studied, members of the Big Three automakers, especially GM, wanted to add automation to their manufacturing lines. This big capital investment would be offset by the reduction in payroll the new machines would afford when they replaced employees.

Of course the unions resisted, causing GM to rethink their plans. But they determined that the efficiencies they could achieve would actually be greater than the investment *and* the payroll expense of the displaced workers. So something called the "Jobs Bank" was created, where these excess workers were sent to do nothing, at 95% of their former compensation. By the way, the Jobs Bank existed in some form for approximately 20 years.

Think about that: IP in the form of technology created efficiencies that exceeded acquisition costs and legacy payroll. This efficiency through technology is still going on with your big business Customers. As I point out in chapter 24, "Outsourcing: The Mother of Niches," you can't become an integrated partner with larger Customers if you aren't following their IP strategy.

IP in the Age of the Seller

In the Age of the Seller, IP was largely the domain of big business, which adopted every form of IP they could get their hands on. In those days most IP, like patents, licenses, and trade secrets, were expensive to create or buy and then make useful. Whether internally created or purchased, large firms had the ability to capitalize the capability that IP delivered, typically in the form of digital technology, even when it cost millions and was crude by current standards. But they had little choice, since automation from IP innovation was, and still is, the primary way large firms find efficiencies to operate their extended organizations and grow in order to maintain market share.

Such was not the case for small businesses in the original Age, where most intangible assets were too expensive, and, therefore, less represented as strategic tools.

IP in the Age of the Customer

All of this started changing with the availability of the Personal Computer. First the Apple II (late 1970s), then the IBM PC (1982), followed closely by the Apple Macintosh (1983). Microsoft Windows (1985) and the PC clones really democratized computer processing power, especially for small businesses, for two reasons: Windows was almost as easy to use as Macintosh, and PC clones were less expensive.

With this newfound micro-processing power, even the smallest of small businesses were given access to three powerful new abilities:

1. Someone else's automation IP was available in diminutive applications and affordable pricing.
2. Acquired IP made it easier to create their own proprietary IP.
3. The new IP power, both acquired and created, allowed them to take advantage of the increasing outsourcing opportunities big businesses were offering, again, as I discuss in chapter 24.

Your IP Strategy

The great IP paradox of the Age of the Customer is that, while small businesses in general have adopted the IP of other businesses, primarily in the form of technology, they tend to think of that activity as just acquiring a new tool that's handier than the last one. But what they should be thinking about is that more and more of their world—Customers and competitors—now exists in a universe where the third asset category, intangible intellectual property, has become the dominant business lever.

Answer these questions to see how you think about IP:

1. If I gave you (a) a truckload of inventory worth thousands or (b) a technology that no one else had that would help you serve your Customers better, which would you choose?
2. Do you spend more and more time (a) thinking about products and services or (b) finding technology and systems to more effectively and efficiently serve and be relevant to Customers?
3. Do your employees (a) use the same technology in the direct performance of their jobs today compared to five years ago or (b) new innovations and more technology?
4. If you were purchasing a business from someone, which would be more valuable to your future success: (a) the inventory and business equipment or (b) the electronic customer information the seller has amassed about the expectations of their Customers?

THIS WILL BE ON THE TEST

Intellectual property is that unique inventory that can be sold repeatedly without being depleted in the process.

Yes, these are trick questions—how did you do?

Just as a key to success in sales is thinking relationship, not transaction, so it is with IP success. Every business must have an IP strategy that is born from the acknowledgement that acquiring and creating IP is integral to the performance of virtually every talent and task your business performs. Some suggestions include:

- Don't think of your new delivery schedule as just a new route for your trucks; it's your proprietary IP that's making your business more efficient and, therefore, more relevant to Customers.
- The systems you've developed to produce products probably seem routine and common sense to you, right? No big deal. Well, it is a big deal, because it's one of the keys to your success. It's an intangible asset you created and are maintaining as a trade secret—your proprietary IP. As such it should be recognized, protected, and defended, just as diligently as you lock the doors of your business at night.

- Don't think of social media IP you acquire from Facebook, Twitter, etc., as something everyone else is doing; this acquired IP is an intangible resource that can create very tangible customer Communities.
- Connect members of Communities you build on acquired social media IP with your face-to-face Communities (customer list) by developing proprietary IP that integrates these two groups.
- Don't just acquire customer relationship management (CRM) and email marketing from other companies. Create your own proprietary IP strategy that combines your virtual and face-to-face contact strategies to help you serve and maintain relevance with Customers.
- Don't think of buying another computer to replace the last one; acquire a processing tool that, among other things, is the device from which your IP strategy is controlled, as it puts you in a position to maximize time, energy, and resources.

THIS WILL BE ON THE TEST

Systems you've developed and are maintaining as a trade secret are your proprietary IP.

It's not my job to tell you step-by-step how to create your own IP strategy. Essentially all proprietary intangible assets begin as a trade secret, and most remain that way. So by definition, small business IP development is as unique as belly buttons. My job is to get your head out of the tangible sand enough that you start thinking about the increasing power of intangible assets, regardless of the source.

We're not going to abandon tangible assets—we'll need those for a long time. But let's put them in the proper proportion, closer to the ratio found in Krosin's research, which proved that the asset-leverage Rubicon has been crossed: the alpha member of the asset classes is now IP.

BLASINGAME'S LAW OF ASSET HIERARCHY

The tangible assets we use in the Age of the Customer, will increasingly be determined by IP innovations.

How Do You File a UCC on a Website?

Let's talk about how small businesses fund this increasing growth and dependence upon IP.

In the marketplace, the Golden Rule goes like this: He who has the Gold makes the Rules. And nowhere in the marketplace is this truer than in the relationship Sellers have with banks when they want to acquire a business loan.

When a Seller borrowed money from a bank to buy an asset in the original Age, it was likely something that had some kind of legal description or identifier that could be recorded at the courthouse in the borrower's county of residence. A bank secures real estate by recording a mortgage, complete with legal description, and a truck or computer is secured as collateral by filing a Uniform Commercial Code (UCC) financing statement, complete with the vehicle identification number (VIN) or a serial number.

This worked great when most assets were tangible. But as we now know from the Krosin research and our own experience, more and more assets don't have legal descriptions or serial numbers. So here is a very important Age of the Customer question: How does a bank file a UCC on a website? Of course, in this case, "website" is a metaphor for IP.

THIS WILL BE ON THE TEST

Developing your IP strategy is a marathon, not a sprint.

In almost every way, the Age of the Customer is not only good for small businesses that understand that there has been a paradigm shift, but it actually creates many advantages not available in the original Age. Flexibility, versatility, granularity, authenticity, transparency, humanity, customization, incrementalization, values, and the ability to identify, respond to, and deliver relevance to Customers at the Moment of Relevance, thy name is small business. Congratulations.

But one of the challenges the new Age is creating for small businesses is the ability to borrow working capital to fund the acquisition of tools they need to grow, when more and more of those assets are intangible, digital IP. Banks love serial numbers and legal descriptions, and they can find neither in the binary code.

Here are four things that will happen regarding the funding of IP as the inversion of asset classes becomes fully diffused in the small business sector:

1. Working capital from outside sources, like angel investors and crowdfunding, will increasingly become capitalization options for small businesses.

2. Retaining earnings will become a more important operating discipline than ever, because IP you can pay for with profits doesn't have to be financed.
3. With a stronger balance sheet from retained earnings, a small business will become more credit-worthy for transactions that don't include legal designations.
4. Banks will ultimately find a way to create a loan product strategy that allows for secured transactions without a legal designation.

Now that you've been forewarned about the dynamics of funding IP, start thinking about and executing an IP capitalization strategy that includes all of these points. Be patient. This is not a sprint; it's a marathon.

Prepare for the Moment of Relevance

My experience shows that most small businesses are pretty good at acquiring and adopting someone else's intellectual property. And often, the problem isn't that small businesses aren't creating proprietary IP. But rather, the challenge is:

- Acknowledging the growing impact of IP as a powerful lever for businesses of all sizes.
- Recognizing, valuing, and employing to the fullest advantage the intangible assets you create.
- Developing an IP strategy that adopts acquired IP and proprietary IP, as well as looking for opportunities to integrate the two.

> **THIS WILL BE ON THE TEST**
>
> *IP strategy is now more about matching your innovations with customer expectations than beating the competition.*

In the Age of the Seller, IP was used to gain a competitive advantage. In the Age of the Customer, a robust and comprehensive IP strategy is more about matching your innovations with customer expectations to achieve relevance than beating the competition. And the same technological innovations that created those new expectations simultaneously afford small businesses the new tools and resources to be innovative enough to turn disruptions into opportunities.

Intellectual property is that unique inventory that can be sold repeatedly without being depleted in the process. But as Microsoft founder, Bill

Gates, once warned, "Intellectual property has the shelf life of a banana." Consequently, at the heart of proprietary IP is innovation, and the essence of a proprietary IP strategy is continuous innovation. And more than that, Age of the Customer forces will require you to create a culture of innovation, where innovation is a way of life, not just a means to an end. Indeed, gaining and maintaining relevance with Customers will dictate constant innovation. And whether great or small, granted by the government or confidential, whenever you innovate you create some form of IP.

Someone has to be the leader of all of this innovation and IP creation. Who's doing that in your organization? Who's making sure that your innovation adoption and creation is helping you maintain relevance with Customers?

In the Age of the Customer, advantage goes to Sellers that leverage intellectual property more and tangible assets less.

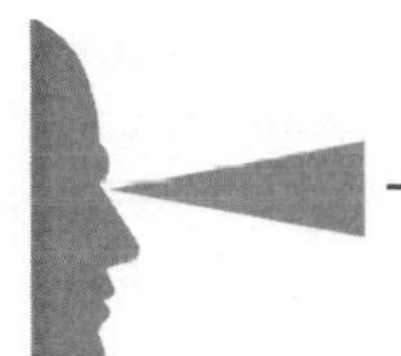

Chapter 21

Your Future in the Cloud

Cloud computing is a better way to run your business.

—Marc Benioff
Founder & CEO, Salesforce.com

Clouds have always been part of human existence, but the phrase, "in the clouds" is more recent.

In aviation, pilots use "in the clouds" to describe actual flight conditions. But it's also used metaphorically, as you might hear a parent's lament about where their teenager's head is. But in the Age of the Customer, it has found a place in the marketplace vernacular referring to where computing power resides. And it's a very real way to grow your business more efficiently and find customer relevance.

Cloud computing is the availability of incremental processing power that resides not on your hard drive, but on someone else's servers that you link up with online, "in the cloud."

If you've ever made a transaction on eBay or paid with PayPal, you've done business in the cloud. When you joined a social media site or attended a webinar, you were in the cloud. When you purchase an agreement to have another company provide up-to-date protection from malware for your computer, you're a cloud customer.

The term *cloud computing* is newer than the capability. The early term was ASP, or Application Service Provider. These were the first developers of processing power accessed over the Internet where customers didn't own it or install it on a hard drive. For example, Hotmail was a free ASP and Salesforce.com was an early fee-based ASP.

The next generation of this highly efficient way to leverage technology was—and still is—software-as-a-service (SaaS). These are typically more sophisticated programs. That computer security contract mentioned earlier is an example of SaaS. When IBM famously reinvented itself with a greater focus on services, SaaS ultimately became one of its primary delivery methods.

Today there are a gazillion SaaS products available, all delivered in the cloud. More and more, acquiring processing power over the Internet has become the norm rather than an option for managing your work and life in cyberspace. And for small businesses, the cloud is the next generation of gaining and maintaining computer processing power, operating efficiencies, and customer relevance. Here's why.

> **THIS WILL BE ON THE TEST**
>
> *Become more aware of how to use the cloud for growth and profitability strategies.*

Virtually by definition, cloud computing means incremental delivery, on-demand availability, and pay-as-you-go pricing. No muss, no fuss, and turn around on a dime—just like a small business and just what small businesses need. The more a small business can acquire processing power online, the less it has to commit precious capital to own that power.

Now let's talk about how the cloud can benefit you directly.

Taking the Cloud to Market

One of the greatest human developments is the marketplace. Webster defines it as a place where goods and services are offered for sale.

Historically, as trade expanded markets, products led the way, because services were difficult to convey to the last mile of consumption. But technology has helped services catch up, and now digital services are delivered efficiently in the cloud. And more than anything else, this last reality is helping small businesses compete and grow in ways that were formerly the domain of larger companies.

Over millennia, innovations took markets from local to global, and now to the Age of the Customer iteration—virtual markets. And virtual markets are powered by cloud computing.

It's likely your business uses cloud resources more than you realize. But with all of the cloud power available, every small business should become more aware of how to use the cloud for their growth and profitability strategies. Here are five cloud-based resource categories that will help you operate more efficiently, maintain competitiveness, grow profitably, and, most importantly, achieve and maintain customer relevance.

The Power of the Cloud

Processing Power

Robust SaaS can be purchased incrementally and accessed as needed. SaaS advantages include increased capability, most recent updates, and expensing instead of capitalizing.

Information Power

Cloud-based communication, Customer development, Community building, and financial applications help small businesses acquire and manage information quickly and strategically.

Sales Power

Cloud-based e-commerce has never been easier or more cost-effective for small businesses to offer, sell, and even deliver products and services 24/7/365.

Talent Power

More and more, Age of the Customer jobs don't require employees to be under the nose of management. Cloud-based employee search capability improves candidate acquisition, and cloud-based communication and collaboration tools foster successful virtual working relationships.

Asset Protection Power

Business assets used to be largely tangible, like inventory, equipment, etc. Today all businesses are increasingly creating opportunity from intangible assets. But for small businesses, protecting intangible, digital assets has been problematic. Cloud-based data back-up services work automatically, securely, productively, and cost effectively.

In chapter 24 on outsourcing, I describe outsourcing as allowing someone else to provide a capability that you either don't have, aren't good at, or don't want to manage and capitalize. Well, think of any cloud-based contract you enter into as a kind of mini-outsourcing, because it fits that definition perfectly, except in more bite-size increments.

Prepare for the Moment of Relevance

Cloud computing has become one of the great providers of efficient and affordable processing power for small businesses. Thanks to the cloud, we've become faster, smarter, more versatile, and more financially viable as integrated partners to our Customers.

As established previously, being competitive is still important in the new Age. And you will easily seek out and recognize cloud services as opportunities to gain a competitive advantage. But now I want you to add a new specification to your adoption of cloud-based capability with this question: "How can the cloud make my business more relevant to Customers?"

The answer is that there are as many different ways—and unique combinations—as there are Sellers and Customers. My job is not to point out all of the ways you can find relevance in the cloud, but to point out that you can find customer relevance in cloud-based capability.

By adopting and using cloud computing resources, you can find, acquire, and stay closer to Customers, which will help you achieve sustainable and profitable business growth.

In the Age of the Customer, your future will increasingly be found in the cloud. But, as powerful as it may be, and as you will see in the following chapter, the cloud does have limitations.

Chapter 22

No Handshake in the Cloud

Now let's talk about when to come down out of the cloud. No, I'm not contradicting myself from the last chapter. Remember, the cloud is a resource which we use as a means to an end, not a way of life. Sometimes the cloud is not the place to be.

While cloud computing is another example of technology increasing business efficiencies and leverage, like all other high-tech tools, it still hasn't replicated one of the elemental components of the marketplace: the handshake. Let me say that again:

There is no handshake in the cloud.

Successful Sellers have learned how to profit from the speed and efficiencies of e-tools found in the cloud. And those who initially discounted the notion of successful virtual relationships over the Internet have been proven wrong. By now, most of us have met a Prospect, delivered a proposal, closed a deal, delivered as promised, and maintained that relationship, perhaps for years, using nothing more than the virtual connection resources at our fingertips. But sometimes, there's just no substitute for face-to-face, as the following story proves.

After a successful four-year relationship between a small business and a very big business Customer, in which most contact had been virtual, the small business owner wanted to deliver a proposal with a new idea for their relationship. The Customer said, "Sure, I'll take a look; just email it like the last one."

But having met the Customer only once in person, plus considering the importance of this proposal to his business, the entrepreneur asked for a meeting. "If you think it's worth your time and expense, sure," the Customer agreed. The meeting was set and conducted, and the new sale was made. After which the Customer said, "I'm glad you came to see me. I probably wouldn't have made this commitment without your personal presentation."

This story is true. That was my proposal, my customer (Steve Wittenborn with IBM), and my sale.

As you leverage and profit from all of the efficient high-tech customer connection tools at the speed of light, don't forget that the best choice might not always be found in the cloud. Sometimes the best option is to invest the time and resources to look Customers in the eye, shake their hand, ask them for their business, and then thank them face-to-face.

You Can't Hide Behind Technology

Now in its third century and second millennia since Samuel Morse invented the telegraph, communication technologies have sought relevance in an increasingly noisy universe. Today there is actual management pain from an embarrassment of riches of communication options. And this discomfort is especially keen when connecting with Customers electronically: Should you email or text? How about IM? And when should you use social media?

But from telegraph to telephone to Twitter, there has been one constant that has retained its relevancy: in-person connection. As I've said before, face-to-face contact is the original social media.

For Sellers, social media adoption has always needed to be tempered by ROI reality. And as useful as each new communication resource proves to be, they are, after all, merely tools to leverage our physical efforts, not eliminate the basic human need for interacting in person. Here's another story:

> A sales manager (whose gray hair was not premature) noticed the sales volume of one of his rookies was below budget for the third consecutive month. He had questioned the numbers previously but allowed his better judgment to be swayed by plausible explanations. Now there was a downward trend.
>
> Upon more pointed probing, the manager discovered the reason for loss of production: too much electronic contact and not enough face-to-face. The rookie was relying too heavily on virtual tools and missing opportunities to meet with customers in person.
>
> It turns out lack of training and rubber-meets-the-road experience left the rookie uncomfortable and unprepared to ask for and conduct face-to-face meetings, like proposal presentations. Consequently, he wasn't benefiting from how the success rate of growing customer relationships can increase when certain critical steps are conducted in person. This manager immediately developed a training program that established standards for how and when to integrate all customer connection tools, including the face-to-face option.

If your sales could use some help trending upward, perhaps your salespeople need help getting in front of Prospects and Customers, particularly at critical steps, as revealed in chapter 16, "The Rules of Selling Have Changed." Like the manager in the story, you may need to establish specific and measurable standards for when face-to-face meetings should take place.

There is one connection option that has borne witness to all of the others and continues to be as relevant as ever: in person contact.

Just Ask Your Customers

In the Coen brothers' film *Oh Brother Where Art Thou?*, Charles Durning's character, Governor Pappy O'Daniel, was running for reelection during the Great Depression. As he entered a radio station to cut a commercial, one of his aides asked him about campaigning face-to-face and "pressin' the flesh." The governor rebuked the man with, "We're not one-at-a-timin' here, we're mass communicatin'!"

> **THIS WILL BE ON THE TEST**
>
> *There has been one constant that has retained its relevancy: in-person connections.*

As Governor Pappy discovered, fancy innovations have created great leverage and efficiencies. But with all of our new telecom and online options, is it possible to have too many? Don't kill the messenger for suggesting that sometimes there is no substitute for one-at-a-timin' it. Indeed, as we adopt and use the next new connection tool to our advantage, please do so with John Naisbitt's enduring prophesy in mind: "The more high tech we have, the more high touch we will want."

There is a solution that can take away most, if not all, of the which-tool-should-I-use pain. In fact, it's available right under your nose, completely intuitive, wonderfully effective—and free, as this true story reveals:

> There was a salesperson—a man who was pushing the upper limits of the Baby Boomer envelope—who couldn't understand why one of his customers—a woman squarely in the middle of Generation Y—wasn't returning his calls or emails about a proposal he had sent her. One day, a colleague suggested he send her a text message and showed him how. As the two friends were still talking, the salesman was stunned when he received a response text from his customer in less than five minutes.

This salesperson overlooked the magic remedy that would have alleviated his pain. It was right in front of him and it is right in front of us: Ask Customers how they prefer to be contacted and receive information.

So instead of obsessing over high tech or high touch when connecting with Prospects and Customers, try this two-step approach:

1. Determine which option best suits the circumstance. One time a proposal can be delivered by high tech email, next time it might be more effective to deliver it with high touch—in person.
2. Ask Customers how they want you to connect with them. You'll find that life and business is so much easier when you just ask Customers what they want. And nothing bad will happen if you suggest the face-to-face option to a Customer.

"It's called network, not netplay."

I began broadcasting my radio program in the 20th century, in 1997. One of the first topics I introduced was three things that small business owners were going to have to be really good at in order to be successful in the 21st century.

1. Adopting technological innovations
2. Building strategic alliances
3. Networking (in 1998, that meant face-to-face)

Of course, my first point increasingly became self-evident and, indeed, is at the heart of Age of the Customer forces. Point two has become more natural for small businesses, as I will cover more in chapter 24. B2B Sellers, especially, have learned that joining forces to share compatible assets and co-bid projects through formal and informal strategic alliances is a great way to play at the next level, even if temporarily.

THIS WILL BE ON THE TEST

Remember, face-to-face is the original social media.

But the third point, face-to-face networking, has been somewhat under pressure—in no small part due to the advent of social media. If you can "meet" lots of people online, the argument has been made, why travel to a physical place to network with a few people?

But not so fast. Let's review.

- In chapter 6, "The Influencers," I introduced the increased role that Communities will play in the future of your business. You can't have too many Communities, including those you develop and maintain face-to-face. Consider ...

BLASINGAME'S NEW LAW OF NETWORKING

Networking = Community = Customers

- In chapter 7, "Value and Values," the power and importance of your personal and corporate values were introduced. It's possible to demonstrate values in an online relationship. I've done it. But there's no more powerful way to do this than face-to-face.
- In chapter 16, "The Rules of Selling Have Changed," I demonstrated how Prospects now require a greater demonstration of relevance from Sellers before they allow a first meeting. In Step One, the most successful Sellers will find a way to get face-to-face with the Prospect through the practice of professional networking.

The best evidence I can offer you as to the increased value of face-to-face networking in the Age of the Customer is with this true success story.

Ivan Misner, Ph.D. is the Founder and Chairman of BNI (Business Network International). In 1999, he joined me on my radio program for the first of dozens of times since. BNI's model is to form local chapters where business professionals gather every week to network face-to-face. Each BNI chapter is a community that promotes the development of customer communities. By the way, the title of this section is a classic quote from Ivan.

In 1999, BNI was a few years old and had several hundred chapters inside the U.S. and a few in other countries. In the intervening years, BNI has grown to thousands of chapters all around the world. And all of this growth happened even as Age of the Customer virtual forces have been the most dramatic. Face-to-face networking is still powerful and relevant.

Perhaps the great paradox of this book is that while virtual technology is powering the Age of the Customer, face-to-face, as a practice, continues to be evident, relevant, and successful.

Prepare for the Moment of Relevance

When I started out in the marketplace, everyone connected the same way, regardless of age or background: phone, face-to-face, or snail mail. When you connected, you called, mailed, or went to a place, not a person. And the connection method you chose was based on the application or timing, not because of the recipient's preference. Today many calls, and all texts and emails, go to a person who receives it wherever they are. Essentially the only connection option that's fixed is when you meet someone face-to-face.

In the old days, a Seller would be competitive by adding extra phone lines so a Prospect or Customer never got a busy signal. Today, your relevance goal is to identify and comply with a Prospect's or Customer's connection preference.

In the history of the workplace, there have never been as many different generations working full-time as we have today. But that's not all: Unlike any other time in history, each generation has a favorite connection method. I like email, you like to receive a text message, and everyone else prefers their favorite social media platform.

The marketplace—and your Customers—are moving very fast. You can't be relevant to Customers if you're always one or two steps behind them. If you want to at least stay abeam of Customers so your connection attempts are received and considered as soon as possible, you have to discover and use their connection method of choice.

The good news is our technology gives us many handy options to stay close to Customers. The challenge is we have to learn how to manage these options so that we accomplish our goals while maintaining relevance with our Customers.

And remember, face-to-face will always be the original social media.

Chapter 23

Quality Process Trumps Quality Service

The mason who builds a house which falls down and kills the inhabitant shall be put to death.

—King Hammurabi
Ruler of Babylonia, 3,000 BC
From the Code of Hammurabi

As King Hammurabi demonstrates, the concept of quality as a desirable practice has been around for a long time. Five millennia later, in the latter half of the 20th century, being able to demonstrate dependable quality became a quantifiable, predictable, and, therefore, marketable achievement.

Dr. W. Edwards Deming is considered the father of modern quality thinking. He proved that by continually improving the process as it's in progress, you improve not only the quality of the finished product, but also with fewer defective units, both of which drive profit right to the bottom line.

Perhaps Deming's most dramatic success story came from his work in Japan. Following World War II, Deming helped Japanese companies use his quality approach to manufacturing to convert "Made in Japan" from being synonymous with cheap to a global expectation of quality and excellence.

Simultaneous with the Japanese conversion, American companies—most notably, the Big Three car companies, Ford, GM, and Chrysler—disregarded the quality process approach and by the early 1980s had lost significant market share in the United States to Japanese companies like Toyota, Nissan, and Honda, due to glaring differences in the quality of the cars.

One of the keystone concepts of Deming's philosophy was, and still is, to incorporate the input of all stakeholders in the quality process: management, rank-and-file workers, vendors, and even Customers. He even went so far as to empower workers with the ability to stop a manufacturing line if they could identify a quality compromise in the process that could be improved.

Obviously, this kind of empowerment gets expensive in an operation that isn't devoted to quality. But Deming proved that where the quality process is the coin of the realm, empowerment engenders pride, pride produces quality, and quality results in performance, profits, and sustainability.

This quality process was typically associated with large companies, especially the manufacturing sector, which made the organizational adjustments, investments, and training required to achieve a certification by, for example, the International Organization for Standardization (ISO). Standards like ISO became valuable—but expensive—credentials to achieve. An ISO certification included in a bid or proposal told a Prospect that this vendor could accomplish a sophisticated operational handshake. Conversely, no quality certification often meant that a bidder had failed to meet the specifications and would not be allowed to submit a bid.

But what about small businesses?

The Quality Process and Small Business

In the next chapter, I'll explain how, during the latter part of the 20th century, big businesses began relying increasingly on small suppliers and vendors to support them in their non-core competency tasks. As this practice grew and improved, it was only natural that small vendors soon became critical vendor-partners, integrated into their larger customers' operation and supply chain. But achieving integration created issues when it came to quality process standards.

> **THIS WILL BE ON THE TEST**
>
> *The quality process begets empowerment, which engenders pride, which produces quality, which results in performance, profits, and sustainability.*

In the 1980s and 1990s, during the height of the early emphasis on quality certification, I was a consultant and advisor to small business CEOs, including many who were suppliers to manufacturers. Perhaps our greatest quest was to find a happy medium between 1) making the expensive and time-consuming investment in full quality certification; and 2) demonstrating to customers that we had installed the quality process to the degree that we could adequately make that handshake mentioned earlier, without certification.

Because of the time and investment required—many months, thousands of man-hours, and tens of thousands of dollars—it was difficult for smaller firms to justify achieving a quality certification. However, it was completely possible and affordable for them to assume and install Deming's quality process philosophy of continual improvement. That only required a change in thinking and applying certain quality process steps, like empowering employees to fix problems during the process, for example.

While helping my small business clients make this journey through what became a kind of quality craze, I came to understand the difference between a classic, self-proclaimed credential—quality service—and the accomplishment that became that happy medium—installing and demonstrating a quality process.

THIS WILL BE ON THE TEST

Quality service is not the same as a quality process.

Quality Service vs. Quality Process

Quality service is a term businesses have used to declare a commitment to diligent customer support. But in the Age of the Seller, Customers typically associated it with, and businesses too often tolerated it as, promptly addressing a problem. Here's what quality service often sounded like:

"We're sorry that part was the wrong size. But we're committed to quality service, so one of our trucks will be there in an hour with the correct part."

In the Age of the Seller, the flurry of activity (read: drama) associated with this kind of quality service likely impressed the Customer. But while prompt attention is admirable, it's not optimal, because it has a negative impact on sustainability in at least two ways: 1) the Customer was inconvenienced by inaccurate service; 2) having to fix an avoidable problem is the worst kind of profit-eating inefficiency.

Successful customer service is the process of delivering value to a Customer in exchange for payment. Surely this is the prime directive of any business. But this process isn't truly successful unless the relationship can be sustained; and only a quality process produces sustainability.

Quality service is reactionary, while the quality process is proactive. Quality service is often high drama, while the quality process produces no drama. Quality service often means someone is going to get reprimanded, while the quality process means someone is likely to be recognized for excellence.

Executing a quality process, put simply, is serving Customers right the first time. Accomplishing a quality process ranges from the very basic—accurate order filling—to the more complex plan of integrating into your operation only those vendors that share your quality process commitment.

The optimal goal of your quality process is sustainability through profitable customer relationships. This is accomplished when Customers return to find your profitable business is still there, ready to serve them successfully—again.

Quality service—fixing what you didn't do right the first time—may have been sustainable in the Age of the Seller, but it was never profitable. In the Age of the Customer only the quality process—doing the job right the first time—is sustainable, especially for small businesses.

Prepare for the Moment of Relevance

Even if your company's financial condition can withstand the inefficiency of quality service, your brand likely won't.

Several times earlier I've explained how, in the Age of the Customer, other people co-own your brand message through the ability to publish comments (remember UGC?) about their experience with your company. So if a Customer goes to Yelp.com to report that your company was quick to fix what you didn't do right the first time, and another person reports that a competitor consistently got it right the first time, who is the Prospect reading those comments going to call first?

The reason we say "Cash is king," is that the impact of negative cash on a business can be so damaging that it will take your breath away. And profit is queen only because the manifestation of negative profit takes longer to be felt than negative cash, which is the only reason quality service has ever been tolerated as a business practice.

> **THIS WILL BE ON THE TEST**
>
> *In the Age of the Customer, only the quality process is sustainable—especially for small businesses.*

When you're ready to stop tolerating profit-eating quality service and convert to the profit-making quality process, I recommend you start with the book *Managing for Quality*, by my friend and Brain Trust member, Leslie Kossoff, plus her subsequent work on this topic. Leslie does a great job of helping small businesses convert to a quality process. Remember, the quality service you're so proud of may be admirable, but when delivered in response to something that was avoidable, it assaults profitability, threatens sustainability, and, therefore, ultimately could put you out of business.

Convert quality service into the profitable—and sustainable—quality process.

In the Age of the Customer, only the quality process is sustainable, because Prospects will evaluate your "did it right the first time" performance, at the Moment of Relevance, before you even know they exist.

BLASINGAME'S LAW OF THE QUALITY PROCESS

The quality process begets empowerment, which engenders pride, which produces quality, which results in performance, profits, and sustainability.

Outsourcing is the best thing to happen to small business since the personal computer.

—Jim Blasingame

Chapter 24

Outsourcing: The Mother of Niches

The greatest improvement in the productive powers of labour, and the greater part of the skill, dexterity, and judgment with which it is anywhere directed or applied, seem to have been the effects of the division of labour.

—Adam Smith
The Wealth of Nations (1776)

Two dramatic periods during the Age of the Seller were the Agricultural Revolution and the Industrial Revolution. In overtaking the former, the latter ushered in the opportunity for proto-entrepreneurs to create large companies which needed the services of many employees to build the factories and then the products of those factories.

For most of the 19th and 20th centuries, businesses founded by entrepreneurs like Carnegie, Vanderbilt, and Ford, for example, could only grow by the physical expansion of more buildings and factories and hiring more people to work in them. Thus, the major corporation model was born, and virtually every industry produced thousands of these firms that hired millions of employees.

If you visited one of these operations 40 years ago, all the people you saw there would be employees of that company. Of course, management and factory workers were employees, but so was the man mowing the yard, the man painting the wall, the receptionist, as well as the supply clerk—all employees with benefits.

During this period, some small businesses grew into big ones—Ford Motor Company was founded in Henry's garage, and Sears was founded when Richard placed a single ad to sell a watch and deliver it by mail. But in terms of history's treatment of this period, small businesses were essentially considered inconsequential Mom & Pop storefronts on Main Street, of no particular significance with regard to economic or employment impact.

Then something happened that did not end the viability of major corporations, but did adjust their employment practices: employee downsizing, one of the great workplace phenomena of the 20th century. There were three conditions that largely gave rise to and perpetuated this practice in the U.S.:

- The recession of 1973–75
- The subsequent stagflation (high inflation and low economic growth) in the second half of the 1970s and extending into the 1980s
- The double-dip recessions of 1980 and 1981–82

Prior to these influences, there had been a paternalistic attitude in many big companies. Sure, there had been layoffs before, but those were mostly cyclical and, indeed, were often termed "furloughs," meaning the employee expected to be recalled to work in the foreseeable future. Especially for most of the 20th century, if you had a job with a big company, you were not only pretty well taken care of, but you could also expect to retire from the company you hired into out of school.

THIS WILL BE ON THE TEST

Outsourcing is one of the most important things to ever happen to small businesses.

But downsizing was different—major corporations significantly reduced their overhead by cutting payroll permanently. These people weren't being laid off, or furloughed, they were terminated. Moreover, in many cases those positions that were cut were long-time employees. Indeed, the term *downsizing* became synonymous with the termination of senior, tenured, veteran employees, primarily because of the size of their compensation packages.

But just because an employee was removed from payroll didn't mean the work didn't still have to be done. And the realization of this fact gave rise to what I believe is one of the most important things to ever happen to small businesses: outsourcing.

Outsourcing is the practice of contracting with a vendor for the completion of some task that was formerly performed by an employee. It is typically practiced with tasks that are not considered to be one of the core competencies of the company. Let's take a look at a couple of outsourcing scenarios:

Outsourcing Delivery

A manufacturer needs to deliver its products to customers. Instead of capitalizing the purchase of trucks, it leases them from a truck company. This is a contract solution with the outsourcing component being a combination of financial and service. But here's the outsource magic:

In between the company's core competencies of manufacturing and taking care of customers is an important step—long-haul delivery—that is not the core competency of the manufacturer, but is the core competency of the truck vendor's industry. So instead of using its own employees to drive those trucks, the manufacturer asks the truck leasing company to include providing drivers as part of the contract.

Now, with the outsourcing services of trucking professionals, the manufacturer can focus its energy on core competencies. And even though the truck company might be a big firm, it's likely that the truck drivers were supplied through an outsource sub-contract with a small staffing company.

Outsourcing Inventory Management

The same manufacturing company needs supplies, tools, repair parts, etc., to keep the factory working. Instead of capitalizing an inventory of all of these parts, the company contracts with a supply company to provide items as needed from the in-house stock room. Like the trucks in the example above, the company is outsourcing the financial responsibility of the parts until they're needed.

But instead of hiring and training a parts and tools expert, which is not the company's core competency, the company asks that supplier to provide as part of the overall relationship, parts and tools experts to manage, stock, re-order, and possibly even deliver these items to the employee end user. The manufacturer gets the parts it needs, when it needs them, without having to capitalize, manage, or deliver them, and the payroll for those non-core-competency tasks is someone else's responsibility.

By the 1980s, you could start to see the stratification of the marketplace: An unsustainable build-up of corporate employee ranks resulted in downsizing, producing the need for outsourcing those vacated tasks, which spawned the creation of millions of new small businesses, many founded by those who had been downsized. I like to use the word stratification to describe how the adoption of outsourcing created layers of business opportunities. But there is another word that is probably better to use in this case—niches (I prefer "nitch," but some say "neesh"—tomato, to-mah-to).

As outsourcing increased, the marketplace began to stratify, which gave rise to niche opportunities—and Mom & Pop operations started gaining credibility. With the convergence of outsourcing and the coincidental emergence of personal computers and associated software, small businesses started shifting from Main Street storefronts to becoming vendor partners with much larger Customers.

THIS WILL BE ON THE TEST

The finer the niche filled, the more relevant the Seller.

In Praise of Niches

One of the products for which Mr. Sears' company became famous was its Craftsmen tools, especially their mechanical socket wrenches.

Prospective owners of Craftsmen socket wrenches could choose from the classic Good, Better, or Best models. The Best wrench has more notches, or teeth, inside the mechanism, allowing for finer adjustments when tightening a bolt or nut. Plus, in a tight spot, the extra notches make the Best model work, well, best.

For almost 40 years, downsizing, outsourcing, and the influences of the Age of the Customer have caused the marketplace to become like that Sears Best socket wrench; every year, it acquires more notches. But in the marketplace, notches are called niches. And just as more notches in a mechanical wrench allow for finer adjustments, more niches create finer and more elegant ways to serve Customers, which they like—a lot. Indeed, the finer the niche filled, the more relevant the Seller.

As downsizing progressed, so did entrepreneurial niche opportunities, resulting in the most dramatic expansion of the small business sector in history. Did entrepreneurs take advantage of niche opportunities presented to them, or did downsized workers carve out niche businesses to contract for the work they had previously done as employees? The answer is not either/or, it's both/and.

Webster defines *niche* as, "a place or position perfectly suited for the person or thing in it." If there was ever a concept perfectly suited for something, it would be the niche for small business. Indeed, as one small business owner identifies a new niche, another will create a niche within that niche. It's a beautiful thing.

In the future, there will be less mass marketing, mass media, and mass distribution. But there will be more niches—lots of new niches. And while mass business models aren't going away anytime soon, they won't grow like niche models. That's good news for small business and the future of entrepreneurship in the Age of the Customer.

More niches means a healthier small business sector, which I happen to believe is good for the world.

Two Kinds of Outsourcing

The outsourcing stories earlier should cause you to realize that you probably don't have to look very far to find evidence that, directly or indirectly, you're connected to some form of outsourcing and/or niche fulfillment. Indeed, outsourcing has become such an accepted component of the marketplace today that it's often taken for granted.

> **THIS WILL BE ON THE TEST**
>
> *If there was ever a concept perfectly suited for something, it would be the niche for small businesses.*

But I don't want you to take it for granted. I want you to think about outsourcing and filling niches with great interest and intention. For that reason I've identified two ways to think about outsourcing: internal and external.

Internal Outsourcing

Internal outsourcing, a.k.a. insourcing, is when you identify a task your company performs that is not your core competency and contract for those services with another organization that specializes in that task. Just like the big companies who essentially created this practice, look around to see how you can achieve operating efficiencies by contracting for services with an outsource vendor, instead of capitalizing the infrastructure and payroll required to accomplish that work in-house. Here's my recommendation for how to make this happen, and it's all built around what I call …

BLASINGAME'S OUTSOURCING POWER QUESTION

Must this be done in-house?

- Schedule a meeting with your leadership to identify all operating segments or tasks, such as: sales, purchasing, delivery, inventory management, accounting, HR, payroll, benefits, maintenance, etc. Write the answers down on a flip chart or other recording medium.
- Discuss the concept of core-competency, which addresses organizational expertise by segment or task line-item. Typically your core competencies are the things that are most likely to help you add value to Customers.
- Ask the team these two questions: Where are we experts and where are we amateurs? How directly are each of these connected with Customers?
- Schedule a second meeting to discuss these segments further. Ask Blasingame's Outsourcing Power Question: "Must this be done in-house?" Then apply the question even to core-competency items.
- Discuss the answer to these questions and put a "Y" or "N" beside each entry. Don't let the fact that you may not be able to immediately identify a vendor solution impact your decision to create an outsource candidate.
- Move the segments that you've identified as outsourcing candidates to a separate list you can discuss and develop.
- Begin looking for outsource vendors who can appraise your requirements and expectations and deliver a proposal you can compare to your own execution and expenses.

THIS WILL BE ON THE TEST

Internal outsourcing will drive efficiences and improve relevance with customers.

Here are some clarifying questions that should be included in the discussion about whether to outsource any segment or task:

- How much control do we lose, and can we live with it?
- What impact will our decision have on customer relationships?
- How much of our decision to not outsource is about ego?

Remember, any decision to employ internal outsourcing—or not—should be driven by the desire to seek efficiencies and improve relevance with Customers.

External Outsourcing

If internal outsourcing is an operational means to an end of achieving greater efficiency—external outsourcing is a way of life.

External outsourcing describes the business model of the vendors you choose to outsource tasks to. Their business is based on their core-competency being at an expert level, which qualifies them to deliver outsourcing services to you. Examples include: strategic staffing, payroll, accounting, tax preparation, government compliance, inventory management, benefits management, etc. In truth, there are thousands of different ways to deliver outsourcing services because, as we've said, businesses continue to identify and fill niches of niches.

It's important to point out that you could have a business model that traditionally did not provide outsourcing service, but out of which you could make certain elements of the business available as an outsource resource to Customers. Remember the contractor in the earlier story that provided supply and inventory management services associated with the tools and parts it sold to a larger manufacturer? That's a true story about a traditional supply house that previous to the outsource contract, merely delivered their products to the loading dock of the Customer. Today they take the products inside the building, own the items up to the moment of delivery by their personnel and consumption by the Customer, for which they charge a fee on top of the price of the product.

THIS WILL BE ON THE TEST

External outsourcing increases gross profits and relevance.

There are at least two excellent reasons to add this outsourcing component to any business model. By filling that outsourcing niche, they:

1. Create more sales revenue, which will likely have a greater gross profit than the commodity delivered by the service.
2. Separate themselves from other competitors. When you become part of the operation, you've become essentially a vendor partner, probably invited to planning and strategic meetings where no regular vendor would be allowed.

In Praise of Disruption

If it weren't for downsizing, the need for and adoption of outsourcing would not have been as robust. If it weren't for outsourcing, which opened the window for small businesses to meet this demand, there would have been much slower economic output in the past thirty years. When these conditions ultimately converged with personal computers and subsequent Age of the Customer elements, small businesses became increasingly able to deliver outsource services at a higher and more professional level. Once Main Street operations started taking their place as outsourcing vendor-partners and niche fillers, small businesses started gaining credibility as more than just Mom & Pop storefronts.

THIS WILL BE ON THE TEST

Outsourcing is neither a fad nor a trend; it's proven and fully integrated into the marketplace.

If Adam Smith were alive today, he would be excited to see how far we've come in expanding the division of labor concept. From the adversity of downsizing, we got outsourcing and niches of niches, which led to the proliferation of small businesses and the fulfillment of millions of dreams.

Prepare for the Moment of Relevance

The stratification of the marketplace resulted from the need to be more efficient. Big businesses are using the efficiency of outsourcing to focus capital and resources on their core competencies, which are what Customers pay for. In the process, small businesses are becoming those outsource resources and finding new opportunities.

The practice of outsourcing is not a fad. It's no longer even a trend. As a valuable management practice, outsourcing is established, proven, and fully integrated into the marketplace, now all the way out to the last mile of Main Street, where small businesses live.

One of the major relevance markers is how well a company embraces the philosophy of outsourcing as a way to maximize resources and achieve results. Outsourcing alternatives can be critical components of the innovation and creativity applied to solve problems and seize opportunities on behalf of Customers. And the more innovative and creative you can be, the higher margins you can achieve.

Use the power of outsourcing and the niftiness of niches to help you find new efficiencies, business opportunities, and more relevance with Customers.

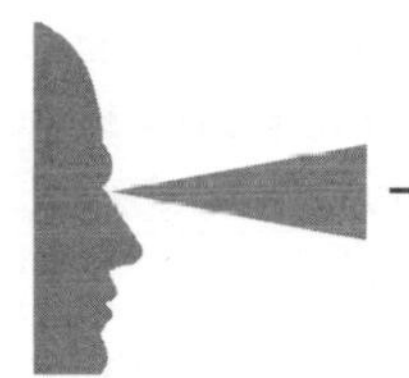

Chapter 25

Globalization In the Age of the Customer

When goods cross borders, armies don't.

—Frederick Bastiat
19th century French economist

In case you haven't heard, the seven-billionth Earthling has been born. And just in time to take advantage of a robust global marketplace, pregnant with opportunities for even the smallest Sellers to do business around the world.

International trade is almost prehistoric. As far back as 1500 BCE, the Phoenicians were perhaps the first to develop and sustain organized trade across geographic and political boundaries.

Traditional international trade has a lot of sophisticated moving parts, requiring expertise, capital, distribution networks, and connections. Consequently, until the Age of the Customer, trade was largely the domain of larger Sellers, due to the significant learning curve and organizational ramp.

But as is the case on so many levels, the new Age has democratized trade opportunities that especially benefit small Sellers. For the first time in the history of the marketplace, it's possible for anyone anywhere on the planet to make a purchase from any Seller in the world and have that item delivered directly to them, whether digitally or physically. More on that in a minute.

Who, Where, and How?

When you put together a strategy to sell products or services delivered outside your national borders, four basic questions have to be asked: 1) Who are my Prospects? 2) Where do they live? 3) How do I connect with them? 4) How do I get paid?

To answer the first two, let's revisit the first statistic in this chapter:

7 billion Prospects. And thanks to an outstanding *National Geographic* article by Robert Kunzig (January 2011), we have a good starting point. Below I've paraphrased a few macro statistics from the article, with my editorializing sprinkled in:

- For American small businesses, 96% of Earth's 7 billion Prospects live outside the U.S.
- For small businesses in the European Union, 92% of their potential Customers live elsewhere.
- Even Chinese entrepreneurs have to look outside their borders to reach 81% of global Prospects, with India's number only slightly more, at 83%. And according to the article, the population percentage of these two will invert by 2030.
- Globally by gender, males barely edge out females: 1.01 to 1.0. But my demographic experts report wide swings in median age among countries, which must factor in any country-by-country trade strategy.
- In a historic shift, just over half of Earthlings are now urbanites. Remember, city folk use different stuff than their country cousins.
- Here are global workplace profiles: 40% of us work in services, 38% in agriculture, and 22% in industry. This means different things to different sectors, but it means something to all Sellers looking for international Prospects.
- English may be the international language of business, but it's the first language of only 5% of global Prospects. When doing business outside their boundaries, English-speaking Sellers must be patient with the translation process as well as being culturally sensitive.
- Breaking news: 82% of your global Prospects are literate. If you can read and write, you can improve your life, which explains the growth of the middle class in emerging markets. And a growing global middle class means more affluent Customers, especially virtual ones.
- Computers and Internet connections are still luxuries for most Earthlings. But now that the cost to manufacture a smartphone is no more than a dumb one, mobile computing is exploding across the globe. Very soon, billions who never owned a PC or used the Internet will accomplish both with a smartphone.

Just as in acquiring domestic Customers, the more you know about who, where, and how global Prospects live their lives will allow you to connect with them on a more informed basis, including identifying their expectations of relevance.

On the traditional global trade front, I've spent decades encouraging small businesses to diversify their growth potential by adding an export/import strategy. The Age of the Customer is helping these traditional transactions with innovations like virtual demonstrations, where Sellers and Prospects hook up with webcams to meet and share information. The virtual presentation innovations of the new Age have significantly reduced customer acquisition time and costs for traditional trade. I encourage any small business to seek out the significant import/export support and resources that are available today.

THIS WILL BE ON THE TEST

Virtual presentation innovations have significantly reduced Customer acquisition time and costs for traditional trade.

Global e-Commerce

Now I want to focus on the big global trade news. The Age of the Customer has created an entirely new global business opportunity: e-commerce.

This new trade capability is arguably the most exciting component of the new Age. First mentioned in chapter 5, "The Moment of Relevance," e-commerce is the nucleus of virtual markets. Here is the basic list of requirements for e-commerce, including answers to the questions about connection and payment.

- Prospects must have access to the Internet.
- The Seller must have a website with product catalog for e-shopping. This is also where Prospects are directed when they respond to traditional or digital marketing efforts. The website must include:
  - An e-commerce user interface, where an offer is made and accepted.
  - Global payment verification and remittance by credit cards, PayPal, etc.
  - Digital IP delivery or physical delivery options for tangible stuff.

Notwithstanding any political issues, e-commerce capability has dropped barriers to entry and truly democratized the ability for even the smallest Seller to seek growth opportunities outside their national borders. The Age of the

Customer has significantly reduced the degree of separation between a Seller and any Prospect on Earth.

Prepare for the Moment of Relevance

International trade is not for every Seller. If you own a local diner, dry cleaner, or home improvement business, you're looking for neighbors, not global Prospects. However, the owner of any of these businesses could write and publish a book that gives insight into operating such a business, or doing business with such a business, and sell the digital version around the world in the virtual market made possible by Age of the Customer innovations.

Many small Sellers do have global opportunities in the virtual marketplace as their primary business model. Plus, remember what I've emphasized throughout this book: the Age of the Customer is simultaneously raining down success opportunities and disruption judgments on the just and the unjust. Take your blinders off and look for trade opportunities and disruptions.

> THIS WILL BE ON THE TEST
>
> *As you focus on sales growth, start looking beyond your borders.*

On the opportunity side, the Moment of Relevance for Prospects outside your country will likely include whether your online presentation and products seem considerate and welcoming of international Prospects. You might even think about having one website for in-country visitors and another one that has more international feel or relevance.

Every Seller, large or small, must keep up with potential threats and disruptions. Just as globalization essentially disrupted the labor factor of manufacturing, the Age of the Customer is shifting *something* in your world. Identify it, understand it, and prepare for it. And remember Blasingame's Law of B2B Relevance: Help your Customers help their Customers. An Age of the Customer disruption or opportunity might not be under your nose, or even your Customers' noses, but if it impacts your Customer's Customers it will impact you.

As you focus on strategic sales growth, start looking beyond your borders for opportunities. Now more than ever before, the information and resources that are available and affordable will help you develop a successful global strategy and execute it successfully at the Moment of Relevance.

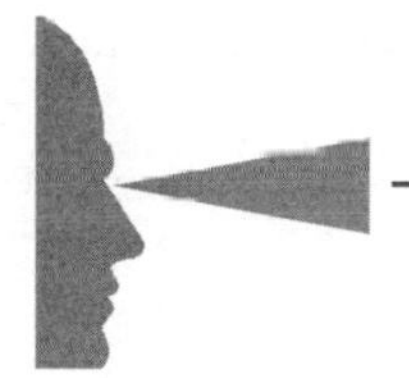

Chapter 26

What Hasn't Changed

What's past is prologue.

—William Shakespeare
from *The Tempest*

Throughout this book I've revealed many shifts with their associated opportunities and disruptions. Now we have to pay homage to things that will not change: timeless fundamentals, both technical and human. Here's the first one.

The Two Most Powerful Words in Business

How much would you pay to own what could be the most powerful way to encourage Customers to come back? Before you get overwrought about how you would come up with the cash for something so valuable, here's the good news: It's free and you already possess it.

There are several versions of this magic gem, each to be used at an appropriate time and engagement, but here's the default version and the most important one:

Thank you.

It was true for thousands of years in the Age of the Seller, and it will be true for all of the Age of the Customer: If your Customers never leave behind their hard-earned cash without hearing a heartfelt "thank you," your business will be a competitive and relevant force to be reckoned with.

Here's an expanded version. Long after this sentiment enters the ears of Customers, when they're considering the next purchase of what you sell, they will remember that you looked them in the eye and transferred these words from your heart to theirs:

Thank you for your business.

Here's one more, in response to a request or when a Customer thanks you first:

It's my pleasure.

And if you really want to pull off the silver-bullet hat trick:

Thank you. It's our pleasure to serve you.
We really appreciate your business.

Saying thank you—and making Customers believe it—forges what I call the Customer Goodwill Alloy. Just as steel is created when you forge iron and coke with other elements, customer goodwill is created when values, commitment, and engagement are forged in the crucible of training, practice, and execution, causing your employees to say "Thank you" every time, with sincerity.

We all know what happens when steel is left exposed and unmaintained: Corrosion causes it to revert to its base elements as rust. But do you know what happens when the Customer Goodwill Alloy is left unmaintained and exposed to the elements? It sounds like this: an employee says "No problem." Or "Here you go." Or "Have a good one." Or even worse, nothing! Not even eye contact!

In the Age of the Customer, where relevance is measured by performance and emotion, you cannot allow your business to revert to customer service rust. More than a means to an end, it must become a way of life to forge and maintain the Customer Goodwill Alloy every hour of every day of every year.

If your door is open, if your phone is ringing, if your website is working, Customers must know how important they are to you. Paraphrasing Paul Simon, there must be 50 ways to express your delight in serving a Customer instead of "No problem." Use them!

"Thank you" has always been powerful and that isn't going to change in the Age of the Customer.

Financial fundamentals

These fundamentals were true in the Age of the Seller, and are just as true in the Age of the Customer.

- As an immediate, operating imperative, cash will always be king.
- As a long-term imperative, sustainable profitability has been, and will

always be, required for business success.

- Retaining earnings is the only way to have growth without debt.
- If you don't charge Customers enough, you won't produce a sustainable gross profit margin.
- If you don't produce and manage with regular and accurate financial statements, you're driving your business 100 miles an hour down a one-way street the wrong way, at night, in the fog, without lights.
- Financial failure and bankruptcy laws are no respecters of marketplace conditions or changes in Customer behavior.

Whatever you knew about financial management of a business in the Age of the Seller is exactly what you have to know and do in the Age of the Customer.

BLASINGAME'S RAZOR

Buy low. Sell high. Keep good records.

Employees Are Still Human

One of the constant themes throughout this book is how much the world has changed and yet how little humans have changed. Yes, technology and innovations have given rise to new expectations, but those are just new practices and conveniences.

Your employees are still people who:

- Are made of the same protoplasm as always.
- Have the same fears, concerns, desires, ambitions, and dreams as ever.
- Want to be successful regardless of their assignment as an employee.
- Expect to feel safe and be safe.
- Desire to be treated with respect, dignity, and honesty.
- Hope to share in the financial success of the organization.

In any Age, Blasingame's Law of Aggregation will serve you well in having engaged, productive, and successful employees serving your Customers:

BLASINGAME'S LAW OF AGGREGATION

Find your success by aggregating the success of your employees.

One of the intangibles that Customers pick up on and are attracted to as a relevance factor is when they come into contact with an employee who is engaged. Of course, if they find unengaged employees, that meeting will produce the opposite effect. This will not change in the new Age.

Prepare for the Moment of Relevance

"Thank you" is music to a Customer's ears. It's the business equivalent of "I love you." Words have always mattered, and as long as humans are your Customers, they always will. Sincerely delivered and felt, I believe "thank you" is more powerful today as a relevance factor than it was when competition reigned.

Business financial failure in the new Age looks exactly like it did in the original one, as does financial success. Consequently, there should be no "the Age of the Customer caused me to fail" excuses. Blasingame's Razor is as simple and relevant as ever.

The value of motivated and engaged employees, who demonstrate that they're invested in the relationship with a Customer, was a competitive advantage in the Age of the Seller and is a powerful relevance factor in the Age of the Customer. Apply Blasingame's Law of Aggregation and find more customer relevance as you first subordinate your own success to the success of your people.

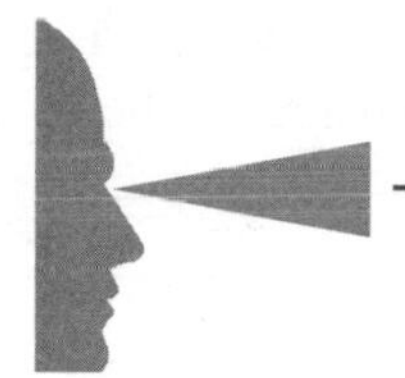

Epilogue

Now You're the Futurist

For time and the world do not stand still. Change is the law of life. And those who look only to the past or the present are certain to miss the future.

—John F. Kennedy

Throughout this book, I've introduced you to at least three futurists who impacted my thinking and, consequently, my life: Joel Barker, John Naisbitt, and Kirk Cheyfitz.

The interesting thing about these three is that they each approach their foresight work differently. Barker is one of the best in the world at providing foresight tools and perspectives that can be used by futurists and regular folks alike, such as his Implications Wheel and paradigm work. Naisbitt is more of a forecaster, as when he so famously and accurately predicted in 1982 that "the more high-tech we have, the more high-touch we will want." And even though he probably doesn't call himself a futurist, very soon after Cheyfitz arrives at one of his unique foresights, he converts it into something useful for the marketplace. Regardless of approach, the product of a futurist's work is foresight.

If I had written this book in my role as a futurist, it would have been published at least 10 years ago, when I first started thinking about these ideas. In that book I would have told you to prepare for the Age of the Customer, and you would likely have been impressed with my foresight.

But since what my foresight would have pointed out then would not have caused you any pain, that book would have been interesting, but likely not useful. The reason is that my foresight would not have identified the active ingredients of the new Age: the way technology is driving customer expectations and the heightened role of relevance. Consequently, the timing of this book is important for two reasons:

1. Enough of the subduction of the original Age by the new one has happened that you can see it and believe it—and your business is likely feeling it.
2. There is still plenty of time to take action and adjust to the new Age before you're run over by it.

Now You're the Futurist

Futurists aren't inspired by God, they're not clairvoyant, nor do they have ESP. But they do look at the world differently than the average person. Futurists rely on big muscles like these to produce their foresight:

- *Foresight tools:* Some sophisticated, some very unsophisticated.
- *Orders of implication:* Like taking a chess opponent's next move out to the second and third possibility.
- *Extreme curiosity:* Beyond the subject of their foresight focus, futurists also cast a wider net to connect the dots of things that are less directly connected to their subject.
- *Collaboration:* They study the work of other futurists, work together, and expose their work to peer review.

Now that you understand how the Age of the Customer is unleashing the power of relevance, it's time for you to become the futurist for your business. Allow me to serve up a compliment with some tough love: No one can be a better futurist for your business than you. You don't have a choice; as the CEO of your business, it's your job.

Let me take some of the intimidation away and make your foresight work easier by converting the list above into plain-language foresight tools:

- *Experience:* Never underestimate the foresight value of past successes and failures (especially the failures).
- *Subject knowledge:* No one is more of an expert on your business than you. Become more of an expert on your industry and related universes.
- *Curiosity:* The only person who's more curious than a futurist is an entrepreneur. Curiosity is one of your most powerful tools—unleash it.
- *Pay attention:* This is the first cousin of curiosity. You pay attention to your business every day, now pay attention to more things outside your four walls.

- *Read:* Professional futurists call it scanning. Read everything you can get your hands on about your industry, your Customers' industries, and their Customers' industries. And that's just for starters.
- *Peer review:* This includes CEO roundtables, whether formal or informal, but it also includes going to industry conventions where you can listen to and compare notes with other operators in your universe.
- *Consider implications:* When you see something happening, unfocus your eyes and imagine the short- and long-term implications. Play the "what if" game with your team on a regular basis. And just like in kindergarten, there are no stupid "what if" questions.
- *Intuition:* This is the love child of experience and curiosity; you have intuition, plus my experts tell me you can grow it. Intuition is educated by experience and employed by curiosity. You can't run your business solely on intuition, but it's an essential component of the foresight discipline of any successful CEO.

Look for:

- Demographic impacts
- Trends in customer behavior
- Trends in production and supply
- Societal trends
- Political implications
- Technology as an opportunity creator and disruptor
- Global events at the macro level that could impact your business at the micro level.
- (Your ideas here)

From now on, as a way of life and not a means to an end, produce foresight scenarios for your business for next year, three years, five years, even the next decade. Apply the foresight tools and parameters—plus those of your own design—to these timelines with questions like:

- Where is my business going?
- Where is my industry going?
- What will my market look like?
- What will happen to my primary customer profile?

- What will my new primary customer profile look like?
- How will I communicate with Prospects and Customers?
- What kinds of products and services will I be selling?
- How will my Customers define relevance?
- Who will be my suppliers?
- How will I capitalize my business?
- What kind of technology will I need?
- What kind of physical plant will I need?
- What will my employee requirements be?
- Where will the greatest opportunities come from?
- Where will the greatest disruptions come from?
- (Your questions here.)

Use the tools, ask the questions, and uncover and prepare for the possibilities that will allow you to take advantage of the opportunities and minimize the disruptions.

Last Thoughts

My singular purpose for this book is to help you get your head out of the Age of the Seller sand and direct your focus on the Age of the Customer reality.

Earlier I introduced you to this quote by Rishad Tobaccowala: "The future doesn't fit in the container of the past."

Let me say that another way:

The way you've done business in the past is not the way you will do business in the future. Of course, you could remind me that this is nothing new.

But here's something that is new:

In the Age of the Seller, you probably knew where your next disruption was coming from, and you could wait until you saw it arriving on the train to make adjustments. In the Age of the Customer, disruptions are coming from places you didn't even know existed, because they might not have existed last year. And they're not arriving on a train; they're being teleported into your world at the speed of light.

Consequently, you don't have the luxury of waiting to change. You don't even have the luxury of managing change. You have the imperative to *lead* change.

Leading change means applying the foresight tools of a CEO to become the futurist for your business. It means you're doing your best to avoid surprises. Even if a surprise turns out well, you still shouldn't celebrate. In fact, you should be just as frightened as if it were a bad surprise, because if a good surprise got through your foresight filters unnoticed until it manifested in front of you, that means a disruption could do the same thing.

Remember:

BLASINGAME'S LAW OF SURPRISES

Surprises are for birthdays—this is business.

Finally, let me leave you with these two thoughts:

Always seek excellence, not perfection.

When opportunity knocks, it doesn't know you've had a bad day.
Greet it with a smile.

Blasingame's Laws

Blasingame's Law of Customer Expectations

Once a new capability or advantage is available to Customers and adopted, that becomes their new minimum expectation.

Blasingame's Prime Marketplace Law

The marketplace is indifferent to your very existence, let alone your survival and success.

Blasingame's Law of Customer Empowerment

When Customers are empowered, Sellers are disrupted.

Blasingame's Law of Relevance

In the Age of the Customer, relevance trumps competitiveness.

Blasingame's Law of Business Love

It's okay to fall in love with what you do, but it's not okay to fall in love with how you do it.

Blasingame's Law of Mobile Computing

Nothing about your past was mobile. Everything about your future will be mobile.

Blasingame's Law of Customer Retention

It's not your Customer's job to keep your business top-of-mind.

Blasingame's New Law of Websites

Your website is becoming less of a destination for customers and more of a distribution center.

Blasingame's Law of Customer Time

In the Age of the Customer, the most important and relevant thing a Seller can do for Customers is to save them time.

Blasingame's Law of B2C Relevance

If you want to have profitable retail Customers for life, give them what they want, not what they need.

Blasingame's Law of B2B Relevance

If you want to have profitable business Customers for life, help your Customers help their Customers.

Blasingame's Law of Selling in the Age of the Customer

Contribute first—contract second.

Blasingame's Laws of Small Business Social Media

1. Your goal is to build online customer Communities.
2. Your prime directive is, "Contribute first, contract second."
3. Your future Customers will increasingly come from Community building activity.

Blasingame's 4 Cs of Storytelling

1. *Connect* to Prospects on an emotional level with a story.
2. *Convey* your expertise, humanity, values, and relevance with a story.
3. *Create* a memory with a story that a Customer will always associate with you.
4. *Convert* Prospects into Customers with the use of stories.

Blasingame's Law of User Interfaces

Never ask a Customer to use your technology unless it's fall-off-a-log easy.

Blasingame's Law of Asset Hierarchy

The tangible assets we use in the Age of the Customer, will increasingly be determined by IP innovations.

Blasingame's New Law of Networking

Networking = Community = Customers

Blasingame's Law of the Quality Process

The quality process begets empowerment, which engenders pride, which produces quality, which results in performance, profits, and sustainability.

Blasingame's Outsourcing Power Question

Must this be done in-house?

Blasingame's Razor

Buy low. Sell high. Keep good records.

Blasingame's Law of Aggregation

Find your success by aggregating the success of your employees.

Blasingame's Law of Surprises

Surprises are for birthdays—this is business.

Bonus Laws

Blasingame's 1st Law of Small Business

It's easy to start a small business, but it's not easy to run and grow one successfully.

Blasingame's 2nd Law of Small Business

It's redundant to say, "undercapitalized small business."

Blasingame's 3rd Law of Small Business

A small business is not a little big business.

Index

Bibliography

Barker, Joel, *Paradigms: The Business of Discovering the Future* (New York: HarperBusiness 1993)

Camus, Albert, *The Myth of Sisyphus* (London: Hamish Hamilton 1955)

Ciancutti, Dr. Arky, *Built on Trust: Gaining Competitive Advantage in Any Organization* (Chicago: Contemporary Books 2000)

Covey, Stephen M.R., *The Speed of Trust: The One Thing That Changes Everything* (New York: Free Press 2008)

Harman, Willis W., *An Incomplete Guide to the Future* (New York: W.W. Norton & Company 1979)

Johnson, Spencer, *Who Moved My Cheese* (New York: G. P. Putnam's Sons 1998)

Kossoff, Leslie, *Managing for Quality: How to Implement and Manage a Business Strategy of Continuous Improvement* (Kossoff Management Consulting 1998)

Kunzig, Robert, "7 Billion," series, *National Geographic* (2011)

Marrella, Len, *In Search of Ethics: Conversations with Men and Women of Character* (Lake Mary, FL: DC Press 2009)

Martin, Chuck, *The Third Screen: Marketing to Your Customers in a World Gone Mobile* (Boston: Nicholas Brealey Publishing 2011)

Naisbitt, John, *Megatrends: Ten New Directions Transforming Our Lives* (New York: Grand Central Publishing 1988)

Poynter, Dan, *Dan Poynter's Self-Publishing Manual: How to Write, Print and Sell Your Own Book* (Para Publishing 2007)

Smith, Adam, *Powers of Mind* (New York: Simon & Schuster 1975)

Smith, Adam, *The Wealth of Nations* (1776)

Solomon, Brian, "The Wal-Mart Slayer: How Publix's People-First Culture Is Winning the Grocer War," *Forbes* (August 12, 2013)

About the Author

Jim Blasingame is one of the world's foremost experts on small business and entrepreneurship. He is president and founder of Small Business Network, Inc., a media company dedicated to serving small business.

Jim is the creator and award-winning host of The Small Business Advocate® Show, the world's only weekday radio talk show dedicated to small business, nationally syndicated since 1997.

He conducts over 1,000 live interviews annually with his Brain Trust, the world's largest community of small business experts, policy makers, and entrepreneurs. Jim reaches a national radio audience, plus worldwide listeners, on his Internet simulcast and the 2600 podcasts produced annually from the radio show (www.SmallBusinessAdvocate.com).

Jim has been a syndicated columnist since 1999, contributing weekly to newspapers and online publications, including Forbes.com, Nasdaq.com, *American City Business Journals,* and OPENForum.com. He has published *The Small Business Advocate NEWSLETTER* every Sunday since November 14, 1999 without missing an edition.

He is the author of two other books, *Small Business Is Like a Bunch of Bananas* (2002) and *Three Minutes to Success* (2006), which have sold almost 100,000 copies combined.

Jim's third book, *The Age of the Customer®* (2014), is being released with 30,000 presale copies. His fourth book, *Technology–As if Humanity Matters™*, will be published in 2015, and his fifth book, *The Third Ingredient™*, will be released in 2016.

Google usually ranks Jim as the #1 small business expert in the world.

In 2009, the American Chamber of Commerce Executives presented Jim with the coveted Champion of the Chamber Award.

The New York Enterprise Report honored Jim with their 2009 Small Business Advocate Award.

The Association of Small Business Development Centers recognized Jim with the 2008 Champion of Small Business Development Award.

The U.S. Small Business Administration recognized Jim as the 2002 Small Business Journalist of the Year.

TALKERS magazine recognized Jim as one of the most important talk show hosts in America.

FORTUNE Small Business magazine recognized Jim as one of the 30 most influential small business experts in the United States.

As a high-energy keynote speaker, Jim talks to small business audiences about how to compete in the Age of the Customer, and he teaches large companies how to speak small business as a second language.

When He's Not Working

Jim is a Rotarian (past president), an ardent supporter of Chambers of Commerce (member of his own Chamber since 1977 and past board member), and he has taught an adult Sunday School class for more than 25 years.

His greatest successes are: daughter, Jenny, who is a Registered Nurse (charge nurse in a CCU) and the mother of two of his grandsons, Jacob and Aaron; son, Craig, who is a police sergeant (SWAT leader, ex-Marine with two tours in Iraq) and the father of two more grandsons, Daniel and Ethan. Jim takes "obnoxious grandfather" to a new level.

Jim wore the uniform of the U.S. Army for 15 years before he resigned his commission at the rank of captain, having commanded an airborne unit for three years in the Reserves. Jim is a licensed pilot with instrument and multi-engine ratings. He owns a set of golf clubs, plays the guitar for his own amazement, and is a wine enthusiast and aspiring gourmet chef.

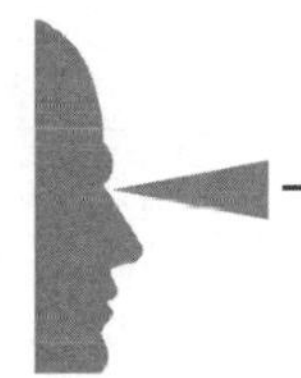

Join the Community

Jim's Websites

AgeoftheCustomer.com: Over time this site will grow and evolve as Jim and the community share information about the impact and influences of the Age of the Customer on our businesses and the marketplace. Please join us.

SmallBusinessAdvocate.com: This is Jim's original website, founded in 1997, where you'll find thousands of easily accessed podcasts, articles, and videos on starting, running, and growing a small business. Everything is available on your mobile devices, too. While you're there, take the weekly poll, sign up for Jim's free weekly newsletter, and visit his blog, JimsBlog.biz.

A high energy keynote speaker

Jim is available to deliver keynote addresses at your meetings and conferences, as well as emcee and panel moderating duties. For more information, contact Davonna Hickman, Vice President, Small Business Network, Inc.: 888-823-2366 or email dsb@jbsba.com.

Corporate Sales

The Age of the Customer is an excellent merchandising gift for customers and clients. Plus we have customization options to offer and will consider your ideas.

For quantity discount pricing, customization, or special fulfillment options, please contact SBN Books.

Toll Free: 888-823-2366

Fax: 256-760-0027

Email: Davonna Hickman, dsb@jbsba.com

Congratulations!

You're now the owner of my third book, *The Age of the Customer*.

Since we know that many people like to read books on digital devices, we've also published this book in all of the popular e-formats.

And here's more good news: You're now entitled to receive a discount off the retail price of our e-book. All you have to do is go to this website ...

www.AgeOfTheCustomer.com

... and type in the code you see below. You'll be taken to a page where you can redeem your discount and download your new e-book.

Discount code: ABA

While there you will also have the opportunity to purchase more hardback copies and/or e-books to send to a friend. And, of course, with appropriate discounts.

Thank you very much for reading my book. I hope it helps you have the maximum opportunity to be successful in your business.